EL ESSENTIALS

—⫻ ON ⫻—

Formative
Assessment

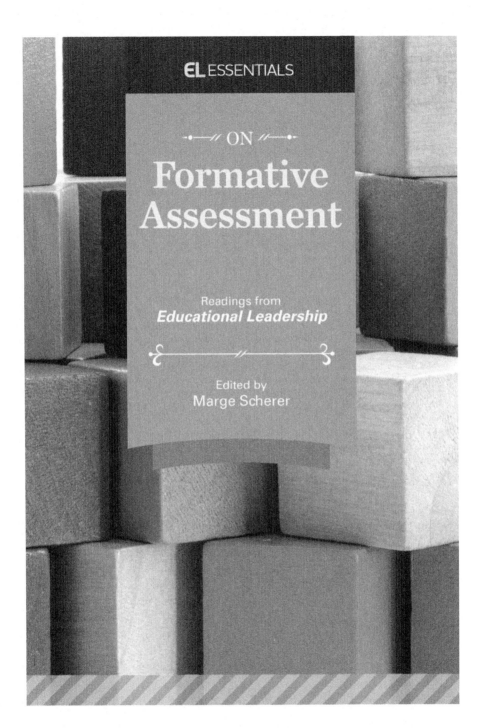

EL ESSENTIALS

—•—// ON //—•—

Formative Assessment

Readings from
Educational Leadership

—c—————//—————ɔ—

Edited by
Marge Scherer

Alexandria, VA USA

1703 N. Beauregard St. • Alexandria, VA 22311-1714 USA
Phone: 800-933-2723 or 703-578-9600 • Fax: 703-575-5400
Website: www.ascd.org • E-mail: member@ascd.org
Author guidelines: www.ascd.org/write

Deborah S. Delisle, *Executive Director*; Robert D. Clouse, *Managing Director; Digital Content & Publications;* Stefani Roth, *Publisher;* Genny Ostertag, *Director, Content Acquisitions;* Julie Houtz, *Director, Book Editing & Production;* Julie Huggins, *Editorial Assistant;* Thomas Lytle, *Senior Graphic Designer;* Mike Kalyan, *Manager, Production Services;* Cynthia Stock, *Production Designer;* Andrea Wilson, *Senior Production Specialist*

Educational Leadership Staff
Margaret M. Scherer, *Editor in Chief;* Deborah Perkins-Gough, *Senior Editor;* Kim Greene, *Senior Associate Editor;* Naomi Thiers, *Associate Editor;* Lucy Robertson, *Associate Editor;* Judi Connelly, *Associate Art Director*

PDF E-BOOK ISBN: 978-1-4166-2230-7   ASCD product #116065E4   n6/16
See Books in Print for other formats.
Quantity discounts: 10–49, 10%; 50+, 15%; 1,000+, special discounts (e-mail programteam@ascd.org or call 800-933-2723, ext. 5773, or 703-575-5773). For desk copies, go to www.ascd.org/deskcopy.

23 22 21 20 19 18 17 16   1 2 3 4 5 6 7 8 9 10 11 12

EL ESSENTIALS

—⫻ ON ⫻—

Formative Assessment

Introduction
Seeing into the Minds of Students

In a way, editors are in the assessment game, scrutinizing authors' work with an eye to selecting the best manuscripts and improving on them, if possible. Sometimes writers tell us that we "read their minds" because we helped them polish their final manuscript. But an editor's kind of assessment is a far cry from the way teachers examine students' work.

Teachers have something else in mind when they use what they call "formative assessment." Their primary aim is to read students, not articles. They assess their students' work to learn what their students know and can do, with the main purpose being to help students to learn on their own.

The practice of assessment has always been part of a teacher's repertoire, but formative assessment has come into its own in the past decade. That's one of the reasons we gathered this assortment of essential articles on formative assessment and feedback, which pulls together some of the best—and most clicked on—articles on these topics that *Educational Leadership* has published.

The articles provide insights into the purpose of formative assessment (Guskey; Tomlinson); the principles to follow for giving the most effective feedback (Wiggins; Hattie; Brookhart; Dweck); and multiple strategies for using effective formative assessment in daily lessons (Wiliam, Duckor, Chappuis, Fisher and Frey, Dueck, and Grdina).

These authors tell fellow educators about how to use formative assessment to shape the next phase of instruction and how to look for patterns in students' assessments and assignments—the mistakes students frequently make, the signals that tell what individuals need, what groups of kids need, what the whole class needs. And they present excellent advice about how to make your feedback more apt to be heard and acted upon by your students.

Whether you are a new or experienced teacher, a school leader, a teacher educator, or a member of a professional learning community, we hope this collection of articles will help you reflect on ways to use assessment to more powerfully boost learning. And be sure to look for new articles in *Educational Leadership* each month as we present the best thinkers in education about topics of most interest to educators. If you have time, we welcome your feedback, too!

—Marge Scherer
Editor in Chief, *Educational Leadership*

1

How Classroom Assessments Improve Learning

Thomas R. Guskey

Teachers who develop useful assessments, provide corrective instruction, and give students second chances to demonstrate success can improve their instruction and help students learn.

Large-scale assessments, like all assessments, are designed for a specific purpose. Those used in most states today are designed to rank-order schools and students for the purposes of accountability—and some do so fairly well. But assessments designed for ranking are generally not good instruments for helping teachers improve their instruction or modify their approach to individual students. First, students take them at the end of the school year, when most instructional activities are near completion. Second, teachers don't receive the results until two or three months later, by which time their students have usually moved on to other teachers. And third, the results that teachers receive usually lack the level of detail needed to target specific improvements (Barton, 2002; Kifer, 2001).

The assessments best suited to guide improvements in student learning are the quizzes, tests, writing assignments, and other assessments that teachers administer on a regular basis in their class-rooms. Teachers trust the results from these assessments because of their direct relation to classroom instructional goals. Plus, results are immediate and easy to analyze at the individual student level. To use classroom assessments to make improvements, however, teachers must change both their view of assessments and their interpretation of results. Specifically, they need to see their assessments as an integral part of the instruction process and as crucial for helping students learn.

Despite the importance of assessments in education today, few teachers receive much formal training in assessment design or analysis. A recent survey showed, for example, that fewer than half the states require competence in assessment for licensure as a teacher (Stiggins, 1999). Lacking specific training, teachers rely heavily on the assessments offered by the publisher of their textbooks or instructional materials. When no suitable assessments are available, teachers construct their own in a haphazard fashion, with questions and essay prompts similar to the ones that their teachers used. They treat assessments as evaluation devices to administer when instructional activities are completed and to use primarily for assigning students' grades.

To use assessments to improve instruction and student learning, teachers need to change their approach to assessments in three important ways.

Make Assessments Useful

For Students

Nearly every student has suffered the experience of spending hours preparing for a major assessment, only to discover that the material that he or she had studied was different from what the teacher chose to emphasize on the assessment. This experience teaches students two unfortunate lessons. First, students realize that hard work and effort don't pay off in school because the time and effort that they spent studying had little or no influence on the results. And second, they learn that they cannot trust their teachers (Guskey, 2000a). These are hardly the lessons that responsible teachers want their students to learn.

Nonetheless, this experience is common because many teachers still mistakenly believe that they must keep their assessments secret. As a result, students come to regard assessments as guessing games, especially from the middle grades on. They view success as depending on how well they can guess what their teachers will ask on quizzes, tests, and other assessments. Some teachers even take pride in their ability to out-guess students. They ask questions about isolated concepts or obscure understandings just to see whether students are reading carefully. Generally, these teachers don't include such "gotcha" questions maliciously, but rather—often unconsciously—because such questions were asked of them when they were students.

Classroom assessments that serve as meaningful sources of information don't surprise students. Instead, these assessments reflect the concepts and skills that the teacher emphasized in class, along with the teacher's clear criteria for judging students' performance. These concepts, skills, and criteria align with the teacher's instructional activities and, ideally, with state or district standards. Students see these assessments as fair measures of important learning goals. Teachers facilitate learning by providing students with important feedback on their learning progress and by helping them identify learning problems (Bloom, Madaus, & Hastings, 1981; Stiggins, 2002).

Critics sometimes contend that this approach means "teaching to the test." But the crucial issue is, What determines the content and methods of teaching? If the test is the primary determinant of what teachers teach and how they teach it, then we are indeed "teaching to the test." But if desired learning goals are the foundation of students' instructional experiences, then assessments of student learning are simply extensions of those same goals. Instead of "teaching to the test," teachers are more accurately "testing what they teach." If a concept or skill is important enough to assess, then it should be important enough to teach. And if it is not important enough to teach, then there's little justification for assessing it.

For Teachers

The best classroom assessments also serve as meaningful sources of information for teachers, helping them identify what they taught well and what they need to work on. Gathering this vital information does not require a sophisticated statistical analysis of assessment results. Teachers need only make a simple tally of how many students missed each assessment item or failed to meet a specific criterion. State assessments sometimes provide similar item-by-item information, but concerns about item security and the cost of developing new items each year usually make assessment developers reluctant to offer such detailed information. Once teachers have made specific tallies, they can pay special attention to the trouble spots—those items or criteria missed by large numbers of students in the class.

In reviewing these results, the teacher must first consider the quality of the item or criterion. Perhaps the question is ambiguously worded or the criterion is unclear. Perhaps students mis-interpreted the question. Whatever the case, teachers must determine whether these items adequately address the knowledge, understanding, or skill that they were intended to measure.

If teachers find no obvious problems with the item or criterion, then they must turn their attention to their teaching. When as many as half the students in a class answer a clear question incorrectly or fail to meet a particular criterion, it's not a student learning problem—it's a teaching problem. Whatever teaching strategy was used, whatever examples were employed, or whatever explanation was offered, it simply didn't work.

Analyzing assessment results in this way means setting aside some powerful ego issues. Many teachers may initially say, "I taught them. They just didn't learn it!" But on reflection, most recognize that their effectiveness is not defined on the basis of what they do as teachers but rather on what their students are able to do. Can effective teaching take place in the absence of learning? Certainly not.

Some argue that such a perspective puts too much responsibility on teachers and not enough on students. Occasionally, teachers respond, "Don't students have responsibilities in this process? Shouldn't students display initiative and personal accountability?"

Indeed, teachers and students share responsibility for learning. Even with valiant teaching efforts, we cannot guarantee that all students will learn everything excellently. Only rarely do teachers find items or assessment criteria that every student answers correctly. A few students are never willing to put forth the necessary effort, but these students tend to be the exception, not the rule. If a teacher is reaching fewer than half of the students in the class, the teacher's method of instruction needs to improve. And teachers need this kind of evidence to help target their instructional improvement efforts.

Follow Assessments with Corrective Instruction

If assessments provide information for both students and teachers, then they cannot mark the end of learning. Instead, assessments must be followed by high-quality, corrective instruction designed to remedy whatever learning errors the assessment identified (see Guskey, 1997). To charge ahead knowing that students have not learned certain concepts or skills well would be foolish. Teachers must therefore follow their assessments with instructional alternatives that present those concepts in new ways and engage students in different and more appropriate learning experiences.

High-quality, corrective instruction is not the same as reteaching, which often consists simply of restating the original explanations louder and more slowly. Instead, the teacher must use approaches that accommodate differences in students' learning styles and intelligences (Sternberg, 1994). Although teachers generally try to incorporate different teaching approaches when they initially plan their lessons, corrective instruction involves extending and strengthening that work. In addition, those students who have few or no learning errors to correct should receive enrichment activities to help broaden and expand their learning. Materials designed for gifted and talented students provide an excellent resource for such activities.

Developing ideas for corrective instruction and enrichment activities can be difficult, especially if teachers believe that they must do it alone, but structured professional development opportunities can help teachers share strategies and collaborate on teaching techniques (Guskey, 1998, 2000b). Faculty meetings devoted to examining classroom assessment results and developing alternative strategies can be highly effective. District-level personnel and collaborative partnerships with local colleges and universities offer wonderful resources for ideas and practical advice.

Occasionally, teachers express concern that if they take time to offer corrective instruction, they will sacrifice curriculum coverage. Because corrective work is initially best done during class and under the teacher's direction, early instructional units will typically involve an extra class period or two. Teachers who ask students to complete corrective work independently, outside of class, generally find that those students who most need to spend time on corrective work are the least likely to do so.

As students become accustomed to this corrective process and realize the personal benefits it offers, however, the teacher can drastically reduce the amount of class time allocated to such work and accomplish much of it through homework assignments or in special study sessions before or after school. And by not allowing minor errors to become major learning problems, teachers better prepare students for subsequent learning tasks, eventually need less time for corrective work (Whiting, Van Burgh, & Render, 1995), and can proceed at a more rapid pace in later learning units. By pacing their instructional units more flexibly, most teachers find that they need not sacrifice curriculum coverage to offer students the benefits of corrective instruction.

Give Second Chances to Demonstrate Success

To become an integral part of the instructional process, assessments cannot be a one-shot, do-or-die experience for students. Instead, assessments must be part of an ongoing effort to help students learn. And if teachers follow assessments with helpful corrective instruction, then students should have a second chance to demonstrate their new level of competence and understanding. This second chance helps determine the effectiveness of the corrective instruction and offers students another opportunity to experience success in learning.

Writing teachers have long recognized the many benefits of a second chance. They know that students rarely write well on an initial attempt. Teachers build into the writing process several opportunities for students to gain feedback on early drafts and then to use that feedback to revise and improve their writing. Teachers of other subjects frequently balk at the idea, however—mostly because it differs from their personal learning experiences.

Some teachers express concern that giving students a second chance might be unfair and that "life isn't like that." They point out that that a surgeon doesn't get a second chance to perform an operation successfully and a pilot doesn't get a second chance to land a jumbo jet safely. Because of the very high stakes involved, each must get it right the first time.

But how did these highly skilled professionals learn their craft? The first operation performed by that surgeon was on a cadaver—a situation that allows a lot of latitude for mistakes. Similarly, the pilot spent many hours in a flight simulator before ever attempting a landing from the cockpit. Such experiences allowed them to learn from their mistakes and to improve their performance. Similar instructional techniques are used in nearly every professional endeavor. Only in schools do student face the prospect of one-shot, do-or-die assessments, with no chance to demonstrate what they learned from previous mistakes.

All educators strive to have their students become lifelong learners and develop learning-to-learn skills. What better learning-to-learn skill is there than learning from one's mistakes? A mistake can be the beginning of learning. Some assessment experts argue, in fact, that students learn nothing from a successful performance. Rather, students learn best when their initial performance is less than successful, for then they can gain direction on how to improve (Wiggins, 1998).

Other teachers suggest that it's unfair to offer the same privileges and high grades to students who require a second chance that we offer to those students who demonstrate a high level of learning on the initial assessment. After all, these students may simply have failed to prepare appropriately. Certainly, we should recognize students who do well on the initial assessment and provide opportunities for them to extend their learning through enrichment activities. But those students who do well on a second assessment have also learned well. More important, their poor performance on the first assessment may not have been their fault. Maybe the teaching strategies used during the initial instruction were inappropriate for these students, but the corrective instruction proved more effective. If we determine grades on the basis of performance and these students have performed at a high level, then they certainly deserve the same grades as those who scored well on their first try.

A comparable example is the driver's license examination. Many individuals do not pass their driver's test on the first attempt. On the second or third try, however, they may reach the same high level of performance as others did on their first. Should these drivers be restricted, for instance, to driving in fair weather only? In inclement weather, should they be required to pull their cars over and park until the weather clears? Of course not. Because they eventually met the same high performance standards as those who passed on their initial attempt, they receive the same privileges. The same should hold true for students who show that they, too, have learned well.

Similar Situations

Using assessments as sources of information, following assessments with corrective instruction, and giving students a second chance are steps in a process that all teachers use naturally when they tutor individual students. If the student makes a mistake, the teacher stops and points out the mistake. The teacher then explains that concept in a different way. Finally, the teacher asks another question or poses a similar problem to ensure the student's understanding before going on. The challenge for teachers is to use their classroom assessments in similar ways to provide all students with this sort of individualized assistance.

Successful coaches use the same process. Immediately following a gymnast's performance on the balance beam, for example, the coach explains to her what she did correctly and what could be improved. The coach then offers specific strategies for improvement and encourages her to try again. As the athlete repeats her performance, the coach watches carefully to ensure that she has corrected the problem.

Successful students typically know how to take corrective action on their own. They save their assessments and review the items or criteria that they missed. They rework problems, look up answers in their textbooks or other resource materials, and ask the teacher about ideas or concepts that they don't understand. Less successful students rarely take such initiative. After looking at their grades, they typically crumple up their assessments and deposit them in the trash can as they leave the classroom. Teachers who use classroom assessments as part of the instructional process help all of their students do what the most successful students have learned to do for themselves.

The Benefits of Assessment

Using classroom assessment to improve student learning is not a new idea. More than 30 years ago, Benjamin Bloom showed how to conduct this process in practical and highly effective ways when he described the practice of mastery learning (Bloom, 1968, 1971). But since that time, the emphasis on assessments as tools for accountability has diverted attention from this more important and fundamental purpose.

Assessments can be a vital component in our efforts to improve education. But as long as we use them only as a means to rank schools and students, we will miss their most powerful benefits. We must focus instead on helping teachers change the way they use assessment results, improve the quality of their classroom assessments, and align their assessments with valued learning goals and state or district standards. When teachers' classroom assessments become an integral part of the instructional process and a central ingredient in their efforts to help students learn, the benefits of assessment for both students and teachers will be boundless.

References

Barton, P. E. (2002). *Staying on course in education reform.* Princeton, NJ: Statistics & Research Division, Policy Information Center, Educational Testing Service.

Bloom, B. S. (1968). Learning for mastery. *Evaluation Comment (UCLA-CSEIP), 1*(2), 1–12.

Bloom, B. S. (1971). Mastery learning. In J. H. Block (Ed.), *Mastery learning: Theory and practice.* New York: Holt, Rinehart & Winston.

Bloom, B. S., Madaus, G. F., & Hastings, J. T. (1981). *Evaluation to improve learning.* New York: McGraw-Hill.

Guskey, T. R. (1997). *Implementing mastery learning* (2nd ed.). Belmont, CA: Wadsworth.

Guskey, T. R. (1998). Making time to train your staff. *The School Administrator, 55*(7), 35–37.

Guskey, T. R. (2000a). Twenty questions? Twenty tools for better teaching. *Principal Leadership, 1*(3), 5–7.

Guskey, T. R. (2000b). *Evaluating professional development.* Thousand Oaks, CA: Corwin Press.

Kifer, E. (2001). *Large-scale assessment: Dimensions, dilemmas, and policies.* Thousand Oaks, CA: Corwin Press.

Sternberg, R. J. (1994). Allowing for thinking styles. *Educational Leadership, 52*(3), 36–40.

Stiggins, R. J. (1999). Evaluating classroom assessment training in teacher education programs. *Educational Measurement: Issues and Practice, 18*(1), 23–27.

Stiggins, R. J. (2002). Assessment crisis: The absence of assessment for learning. *Phi Delta Kappan, 83*(10), 758–765.

Whiting, B., Van Burgh, J. W., & Render, G. F. (1995). *Mastery learning in the classroom.* Paper presented at the annual meeting of the American Educational Research Association, San Francisco.

Wiggins, G. (1998). *Educative assessment.* San Francisco: Jossey-Bass.

Thomas R. Guskey (guskey@uky.edu) is Professor of Education Policy Studies and Evaluation, College of Education, University of Kentucky.

Originally published in the February 2003 issue of *Educational Leadership, 60*(5): pp. 6–11.

2

The Bridge Between Today's Lesson and Tomorrow's

Carol Ann Tomlinson

Formative assessments can improve both teaching and learning, if you follow these ten principles.

There's talk aplenty in schools these days about formative assessment. That's encouraging, because formative assessment has great potential to improve both teaching and learning. Listening to the conversations sometimes, however, reminds me that it's easier to subscribe to a word than to live out its fundamental tenets.

I see formative assessment as an ongoing exchange between a teacher and his or her students designed to help students grow as vigorously as possible and to help teachers contribute to that growth as fully as possible. When I hear formative assessment reduced to a mechanism for raising end-of-year-test scores, it makes me fear that we might reduce teaching and learning to that same level.

Formative assessment is—or should be—the bridge or causeway between today's lesson and tomorrow's. Both its alignment with current content goals and its immediacy in providing insight about student understanding are crucial to helping teacher and student see how to make near-term adjustments so the progression of learning can proceed as it should. I worry when I hear educators say they have purchased formative assessments to give once a quarter or once a month to keep tabs on student achievement. These assessments are not likely to be well aligned with tomorrow's lesson, nor are they able to provide feedback rapidly enough to influence daily instruction.

The best teachers work persistently to benefit the learners in their charge. Because teaching is too complex to invite perfection, even the best teachers will miss the mark on some days, but in general, teachers who use sound formative assessment aspire to the following 10 principles.

1. Help students understand the role of formative assessment.

Students often feel that assessment equals test equals grade equals judgment. That association leads many discouraged students to give up rather than to risk another failure. It causes many high-achieving students to focus on grades rather than learning, and on safe answers rather than thoughtful ones.

It's important, then, for teachers to help students understand that assessments help them learn and that immediate perfection should not be their goal. Teachers can communicate this message by telling students,

> When we're mastering new things, it's important to feel safe making mistakes. Mistakes are how we figure out how to get better at what we are doing. They help us understand our thinking. Therefore, many assessments in this class will not be graded. We'll analyze the assessments so we can make improvements in our work, but they won't go into the grade book. When you've had time to practice, then we'll talk about tests and grades.

It's essential for teachers to help learners both understand and experience the reality that sustained effort and mindful attention to progress feed success. That belief needs to be a cornerstone ethic in the classroom.

2. Begin with clear KUDs.

The first step in creating a worthy formative assessment occurs well before the teacher develops the assessment. It happens when the teacher begins to map out curriculum. At that point, the teacher asks the pivotal question, "What is most important for students to *Know*, *Understand*, and be able to *Do* as a result of this segment of learning?" Absent clarity on the essential knowledge, understanding, and skills for a unit or lesson, the curriculum wanders. But with clarity about KUDs, the teacher is able to focus curricular decisions squarely on what matters most for student success.

KUDs also lay the groundwork for pre-assessment and ongoing assessment. A pre-assessment provides a "dipstick check" of student status as a unit begins. It need not be wholly comprehensive, but rather should sample student standing in relation to the material so the teacher has a reasonable approximation of who may experience difficulty, who may show early mastery, and who may bring misunderstandings to the unit of study. Other formative assessments will follow regularly and often, and together they will form an image of a student's emergent development.

Alignment between KUDs and formative assessments—and later, between formative assessment results and instructional plans—is imperative if formative assessment is to fulfill its promise.

3. Make room for student differences.

The most useful formative assessments make it possible for students to show what they know, understand, and can do; therefore, it's useful for teachers to build some flexibility into formative assessments. For example, a student who is learning English may be able to draw and label a diagram of the relationship between density and buoyancy but not write a paragraph explaining it. The prompt, "Use an example from your experience to illustrate the idea that a person's culture shapes his or her perspective," is more likely to draw a meaningful response from a broader range of students than the prompt, "Explain the relationship between culture and perspective." Likewise, asking students to illustrate how fractions are used in sports, music, cooking, shopping, building something, or another area they are interested in is more likely to be revealing than asking them simply to explain uses of fractions.

In formative assessments (as in summative ones), it's acceptable—and often wise—to allow students some latitude in how they express what they know, understand, and can do. Assessment formats and conditions can vary as long as all forms of the assessment measure the same KUDs.

4. Provide instructive feedback.

Although formative assessments should rarely be graded, students do need useful feedback. Comments like, "Nice job," "I enjoyed this," or "Not quite" don't help learners understand what they did well or how they missed the mark. Feedback needs to help the student know what to do to improve the next time around. For example, it's helpful for a teacher to say, "The flow of your logic in this section is clear, but you need additional detail to support your thinking." It offers a student little guidance if the teacher simply says, "Not quite there yet," or "Weak effort."

When feedback serves its instructional purpose, students are clear about the learning targets at which they are aiming, and they understand that assessments show how they are doing in reaching those targets. They trust that teachers will use the assessments to help them achieve, and they know that there will soon be follow-up opportunities for them to use the feedback in improving their performance.

5. Make feedback user-friendly.

Feedback should be clear, focused, and appropriately challenging for the learner. As teachers, we sometimes feel our job is to mark every error on a paper. Not only is that practice time-consuming, robbing us of time we could more potently use for instructional planning, but a sea of "edits" without clarity about which comments matter most, how they connect, or what to do next is likely to evoke a negative response from a student.

To realize its power, feedback must result in a student thinking about how to improve—the ideal is to elicit a cognitive response from the learner, not an emotional one (Wiliam, 2011). It's seldom useful to send students a message that their work is stellar or that their work is dreadful. Praise and shame shut down learning far more often than they catalyze it. It's more fruitful to straightforwardly share with students their particular next steps in the learning process, based on goals that are clear to teacher and student alike. The teacher sees where a student is in a learning progression and points the way ahead for that student. In other words, feedback is differentiated, pointing each learner toward actions that are challenging but achievable for that learner.

For example, a teacher who is working with students on using sources to support an opinion provides criteria for the effective use of resources for this purpose. In writing an opinion piece, some students may have difficulty synthesizing ideas from multiple resources. A second group of students may synthesize proficiently but rely solely on obvious interpretations of text. To move ahead, the first group of students needs specific guidance on how to synthesize ideas from resources. The second group needs direction in plumbing ideas more deeply. Both groups will receive feedback in the area of using resources to support an opinion, but their feedback will focus on aspects of the skill set that move them to their next step in development.

6. Assess persistently.

Formative assessment should permeate a class period. A great teacher is a habitual student of his or her students. A keen observer, the teacher is constantly watching what students do, looking for clues about their learning progress, and asking for input from students about their status.

These teachers walk among their students as they work, listening for clues about their understanding, asking questions that probe their thinking, taking notes on what they see and hear. They ask students to signal their level of confidence with the task they are doing with thumbs-up, thumbs-down, or thumbs-sideways, for example, to gain a sense of how the class as a whole is faring. They ask students to write answers to questions on whiteboards or to respond with clickers so they can get an in-process sense of how individual students are coming along.

They use start-up prompts to see what students learned from last night's homework. They use exit cards to assess student understanding as a class ends. They spot-check student work with an eye to seeing how students are progressing with a particular skill. They talk with students as they enter and leave the classroom, at lunch, or while waiting for the school buses to leave. They solicit and are alert to parent input about their students' strengths, attitudes, work habits, and goals.

It isn't really so much that these teachers use formative assessments *often*. It's that they do so *continually*—formally and informally, with individuals and with the group, to understand academic progress and to understand the human beings that they teach. For these teachers, formative assessment is not ancillary to effective teaching. It is the core of their professional work.

7. Engage students with formative assessment.

There was a time when doctors examined patients, made diagnoses, and provided treatment plans with limited conversation about their observations or alternative courses of treatment. More recently, physicians have learned that outcomes improve when patients and doctors exchange information and examine treatment options together.

It's easy for teachers to stick with the traditional classroom paradigm that casts them in the role of giver and grader of tests, diagnoser of student needs, and prescriber of regimens. Things go much better, however, when students are fully engaged in the assessment process.

Students benefit from examining their own work in light of rubrics that align tightly with content goals and point toward quality of content, process, and product—or in comparison to models of high-quality work that are just a bit above the student's current level of performance. They benefit from providing feedback on peers' work, as long as the feedback is guided by clear criteria and a process that enables them to provide useful suggestions.

Students also need to be involved in thoughtfully examining teacher feedback, asking questions when the feedback is not clear, and developing plans that specify how they will use that feedback to benefit their own academic growth. Students who are consistent participants in the formative assessment process should be able to say something like this:

> Here are four goals I'm working on right now. In this piece of work, here's evidence that I'm competent with the first and third goals. If we look at my work from a month ago and then at this most recent piece, I can show you evidence of my progress with the second goal. I can also tell you two things I'm going to work on this week to make sure I become more confident and more skilled in working with the fourth goal.

8. Look for patterns.

The goal of reviewing formative assessment is not to be able to say, "Six students made *A*s, seven made *B*s, ten made *C*s, and so on." Neither is the goal to create 32 lesson plans for 32 students. Rather, it is to find patterns in the students' work that point the way to planning classroom instruction that both moves students along a learning continuum and is manageable.

Patterns will vary widely with the focus of the assessment. In one instance, a teacher may see some students who have already mastered the content, others who are fine with computations but not word problems, still others who know how to tackle the word problems but are making careless errors, and another group that is struggling with prerequisite knowledge or skills.

In another instance, a teacher may find that one group of students can provide causes of an event but no evidence for their reasoning, while other students are able to provide both causes and evidence. In still another case, a teacher may see students who understand the general idea being assessed but lack academic vocabulary to write with precision, while other students are using appropriate academic vocabulary. The possibilities are many, but the goal is to look for clusters of student need and plan ways to help each group of students move ahead.

9. Plan instruction around content requirements and student needs.

There is little point in spending time on formative assessment unless it leads to modification of teaching and learning plans. In other words, formative assessment is a means to design instruction that's a better fit for student needs, not an end in itself.

On rare occasions, formative assessment will indicate that everyone in the class needs more practice with a certain skill or more engagement with a particular understanding. Much more frequently, however, formative assessment points to a need for differentiated instruction during at least some of an upcoming class period, in homework, or in both. John Hattie (2012) says that

> teachers must know where students are and aim to move them "+1" beyond that point; thus the idea of teaching the class as a whole is unlikely to pitch the lesson correctly for all students. This is where the skill of teachers in knowing the similarities across students and allowing for the differences becomes so important. (p. 97)

An assessment is really only a formative assessment when teachers glean evidence about student performance, interpret that evidence, and use it to provide teaching that is more likely to benefit student learning than the instruction those teachers would have delivered if they had continued forward without using what they learned through the assessment (Wiliam, 2011).

10. Repeat the process.

Formative assessment is more habitual than occasional in classrooms where maximizing each student's growth is a central goal. In such classes, it simply makes no sense to teach without a clear understanding of each student's development along a learning trajectory. It is wasteful of time, resources, and learner potential not to make instructional plans based on that understanding. Assessment of each learning experience informs plans for the next learning experience. Such an assessment process never ends.

A classroom is a system with interdependent parts—each affecting the other for better or worse. The learning environment, quality of curriculum, use of formative assessment, instructional planning, and implementation of classroom routines work together to enhance student learning—or, if any of the elements does not function effectively, to impede it. Fruitful use of formative assessment is an essential component in the mix.

References

Hattie, J. (2012). *Visible learning for teachers: Maximizing impact on learning.* New York: Routledge.

Wiliam, D., (2011). *Embedded formative assessment.* Bloomington, IN: Solution Tree.

Carol Ann Tomlinson (cat3y@virginia.edu) is William Clay Parrish Jr. Professor and Chair of Educational Leadership, Foundation, and Policy at the Curry School of Education at the University of Virginia in Charlottesville. She is the author of *The Differentiated Classroom: Responding to the Needs of All Learners*, 2nd Edition (ASCD, 2014), and coauthor, with Michael Murphy, of *Leading for Differentiation: Growing Teachers Who Grow Kids* (ASCD, 2015).

Originally published in the March 2014 issue of *Educational Leadership, 71*(6): pp. 10–14.

3

Seven Keys to Effective Feedback

Grant Wiggins

Advice, evaluation, grades—none of these provide the descriptive information that students need to reach their goals. What is true feedback—and how can it improve learning?

Who would dispute the idea that feedback is a good thing? Both common sense and research make it clear: Formative assessment, consisting of lots of feedback and opportunities to use that feedback, enhances performance and achievement.

Yet even John Hattie (2008), whose decades of research revealed that feedback was among the most powerful influences on achievement, acknowledges that he has "struggled to understand the concept" (p. 173). And many writings on the subject don't even attempt to define the term. To improve formative assessment practices among both teachers and assessment designers, we need to look more closely at just what feedback is—and isn't.

What Is Feedback, Anyway?

The term *feedback* is often used to describe all kinds of comments made after the fact, including advice, praise, and evaluation. But none of these are feedback, strictly speaking.

Basically, feedback is information about how we are doing in our efforts to reach a goal. I hit a tennis ball with the goal of keeping it in the court, and I see where it lands—in or out. I tell a joke with the goal of making people laugh, and I observe the audience's reaction—they laugh loudly or barely snicker. I teach a lesson with the goal of engaging students, and I see that some students have their eyes riveted on me while others are nodding off.

Here are some other examples of feedback:

- A friend tells me, "You know, when you put it that way and speak in that softer tone of voice, it makes me feel better."
- A reader comments on my short story, "The first few paragraphs kept my full attention. The scene painted was vivid and interesting. But then the dialogue became hard to follow; as a reader, I was confused about who was talking, and the sequence of actions was puzzling, so I became less engaged."
- A baseball coach tells me, "Each time you swung and missed, you raised your head as you swung so you didn't really have your eye on the ball. On the one you hit hard, you kept your head down and saw the ball."

Note the difference between these three examples and the first three I cited—the tennis stroke, the joke, and the student responses to teaching. In the first group, I only had to take note of the tangible effect of my actions, keeping my goals in mind. No one volunteered feedback, but there was still plenty of feedback to get and use. The second group of examples all involved the deliberate, explicit giving of feedback by other people.

Whether the feedback was in the observable effects or from other people, in every case the information received was not advice, nor was the performance evaluated. No one told me as a performer what to do differently or how "good" or "bad" my results were. (You might think that the reader of my writing was judging my work, but look at the words used again: She simply played back the effect my writing had on her as a reader.) Nor did any of the three people tell me what to do (which is what many people erroneously think feedback is—advice). Guidance would be premature; I first need to receive feedback on what I did or didn't do that would warrant such advice.

In all six cases, information was conveyed about the effects of my actions as related to a goal. The information did not include value judgments or recommendations on how to improve. (For examples of information that is often falsely viewed as feedback, see Figure 3.1 below and Figure 3.2 on p. 30.)

Decades of education research support the idea that by teaching *less* and providing *more* feedback, we can produce greater learning (see Bransford, Brown, & Cocking, 2000; Hattie, 2008; Marzano, Pickering,

---

Figure 3.1: Feedback vs. Advice

▶ You need more examples in your report.
▶ You might want to use a lighter baseball bat.
▶ You should have included some Essential Questions in your unit plan.

These three statements are not feedback; they're advice. Such advice out of the blue seems at best tangential and at worst unhelpful and annoying. Unless it is preceded by descriptive feedback, the natural response of the performer is to wonder, "Why are you suggesting this?"

As coaches, teachers, and parents, we too often jump right to advice without first ensuring that the learner has sought, grasped, and tentatively accepted the feedback on which the advice is based. By doing so, we often unwittingly end up unnerving learners. Students become increasingly insecure about their own judgment and dependent on the advice of experts—and therefore in a panic about what to do when varied advice comes from different people or no advice is available at all.

If your ratio of advice to feedback is too high, try asking the learner, "Given the feedback, do you have some ideas about how to improve?" This approach will build greater autonomy and confidence over the long haul. Once they are no longer rank novices, performers can often self-advise if asked to.

& Pollock, 2001). Compare the typical lecture-driven course, which often produces less-than-optimal learning, with the peer instruction model developed by Eric Mazur (2009) at Harvard. He hardly lectures at all to his 200 introductory physics students; instead, he gives them problems to think about individually and then discuss in small groups. This system, he writes, "provides frequent and continuous feedback (to both the students and the instructor) about the level of understanding of the subject being discussed" (p. 51), producing gains in both conceptual understanding of the subject and problem-solving skills. Less "teaching," more feedback equals better results.

Feedback Essentials

Whether feedback is just there to be grasped or is provided by another person, helpful feedback is goal-referenced; tangible and transparent; actionable; user-friendly (specific and personalized); timely; ongoing; and consistent.

Goal-Referenced

Effective feedback requires that a person has a goal, takes action to achieve the goal, and receives goal-related information about his or her actions. I told a joke—why? To make people laugh. I wrote a story to engage the reader with vivid language and believable dialogue that captures the characters' feelings. I went up to bat to get a hit. If I am not clear on my goals or if I fail to pay attention to them, I cannot get helpful feedback (nor am I likely to achieve my goals).

Information becomes feedback if, and only if, I am trying to cause something and the information tells me whether I am on track or need to change course. If some joke or aspect of my writing *isn't working*—a revealing, nonjudgmental phrase—I need to know.

Note that in everyday situations, goals are often implicit, although fairly obvious to everyone. I don't need to announce when telling the joke that my aim is to make you laugh. But in school, learners are often unclear about the specific goal of a task or lesson, so it is crucial to remind them about the goal and the criteria by which they should self-assess. For example, a teacher might say,

The point of this writing task is for you to make readers laugh. So, when rereading your draft or getting feedback from peers, ask, How funny is this? Where might it be funnier?

As you prepare a table poster to display the findings of your science project, remember that the aim is to interest people in your work as well as to describe the facts you discovered through your experiment. Self-assess your work against those two criteria using these rubrics. The science fair judges will do likewise.

Tangible and Transparent

Any useful feedback system involves not only a clear goal, but also tangible results related to the goal. People laugh, chuckle, or don't laugh at each joke; students are highly attentive, somewhat attentive, or inattentive to my teaching.

Even as little children, we learn from such tangible feedback. That's how we learn to walk; to hold a spoon; and to understand that certain words magically yield food, drink, or a change of clothes from big people. The best feedback is so tangible that anyone who has a goal can learn from it.

Alas, far too much instructional feedback is opaque, as revealed in a true story a teacher told me years ago. A student came up to her at year's end and said, "Miss Jones, you kept writing this same word on my English papers all year, and I still don't know what it means." "What's the word?" she asked. "Vag-oo," he said. (The word was *vague!*)

Sometimes, even when the information is tangible and transparent, the performers don't obtain it—either because they don't look for it or because they are too busy performing to focus on the effects. In sports, novice tennis players or batters often don't realize that they're taking their eyes off the ball; they often protest, in fact, when that feedback is given. (Constantly yelling "Keep your eye on the ball!" rarely works.) And we have all seen how new teachers are sometimes so busy concentrating on "teaching" that they fail to notice that few students are listening or learning.

That's why, in addition to feedback from coaches or other able observers, video or audio recordings can help us perceive things that we may not perceive as we perform; and by extension, such recordings help us learn to look for difficult-to-perceive but vital information. I recommend that all teachers videotape their own classes at least once a month. It was a transformative experience for me when I did it as a beginning teacher. Concepts that had been crystal clear to me when I was teaching seemed opaque and downright confusing on tape— captured also in the many quizzical looks of my students, which I had missed in the moment.

Actionable

Effective feedback is concrete, specific, and useful; it provides *actionable* information. Thus, "Good job!" and "You did that wrong" and *B+* are not feedback at all. We can easily imagine the learners asking themselves in response to these comments, What *specifically* should I do more or less of next time, based on this information? No idea. They don't know what was "good" or "wrong" about what they did.

Actionable feedback must also be accepted by the performer. Many so-called feedback situations lead to arguments because the givers are not sufficiently descriptive; they jump to an inference from the data instead of simply presenting the data. For example, a supervisor may make the unfortunate but common mistake of stating that "many students were bored in class." That's a judgment, not an observation. It would have been far more useful and less debatable had the supervisor said something like, "I counted ongoing inattentive behaviors in 12 of the 25 students once the lecture was underway. The behaviors included texting under desks, passing notes, and making eye contact with other students. However, after the small-group exercise began, I saw such behavior in only one student."

Figure 3.2: Feedback vs. Evaluation and Grades

▸ **Good work!**
▸ **This is a weak paper.**
▸ **You got a C on your presentation.**
▸ **I'm so pleased by your poster!**

These comments make a value judgment. They rate, evaluate, praise, or criticize what was done. There is little or no feedback here—no actionable information about what occurred. As performers, we only know that someone else placed a high or low value on what we did.

How might we recast these comments to be useful feedback? Tip: Always add a mental colon after each statement of value. For example,

• "Good work: Your use of words was more precise in this paper than in the last one, and I saw the scenes clearly in my mind's eye."

• "This is a weak paper: Almost from the first sentence, I was confused as to your initial thesis and the evidence you provide for it. In the second paragraph you propose a different thesis, and in the third paragraph you don't offer evidence, just beliefs."

You'll soon find that you can drop the evaluative language; it serves no useful function.

The most ubiquitous form of evaluation, grading, is so much a part of the school landscape that we easily overlook its utter uselessness as actionable feedback. Grades are here to stay, no doubt—but that doesn't mean we should rely on them as a major source of feedback.

Such care in offering neutral, goal-related facts is the whole point of the clinical supervision of teaching and of good coaching more generally. Effective supervisors and coaches work hard to carefully observe and comment on what they observed, based on a clear statement of goals. That's why I always ask when visiting a class, "What would you like me to look for and perhaps count?" In my experience as a teacher of teachers, I have always found such pure feedback to be accepted and welcomed. Effective coaches also know that in complex performance situations, actionable feedback about what went right is as important as feedback about what didn't work.

User-Friendly

Even if feedback is specific and accurate in the eyes of experts or bystanders, it is not of much value if the user cannot understand it or is overwhelmed by it. Highly technical feedback will seem odd and confusing to a novice. Describing a baseball swing to a 6-year-old in terms of torque and other physics concepts will not likely yield a better hitter. Too much feedback is also counterproductive; better to help the performer concentrate on only one or two key elements of performance than to create a buzz of information coming in from all sides.

Expert coaches uniformly avoid overloading performers with too much or too technical information. They tell the performers one important thing they noticed that, if changed, will likely yield immediate and noticeable improvement ("I was confused about who was talking in the dialogue you wrote in this paragraph"). They don't offer advice until they make sure the performer understands the importance of what they saw.

Timely

In most cases, the sooner I get feedback, the better. I don't want to wait for hours or days to find out whether my students were attentive and whether they learned, or which part of my written story works and which part doesn't. I say "in most cases" to allow for situations like playing a piano piece in a recital. I don't want my teacher or the audience barking out feedback as I perform. That's why it is more precise to say that good feedback is "timely" rather than "immediate."

A great problem in education, however, is untimely feedback. Vital feedback on key performances often comes days, weeks, or even months after the performance—think of writing and handing in papers or getting back results on standardized tests. As educators, we should work overtime to figure out ways to ensure that students get more timely feedback and opportunities to use it while the attempt and effects are still fresh in their minds.

Before you say that this is impossible, remember that feedback does not need to come only from the teacher, or even from people at all. Technology is one powerful tool—part of the power of computer-assisted learning is unlimited, timely feedback and opportunities to use it. Peer review is another strategy for managing the load to ensure lots of timely feedback; it's essential, however, to train students to do small-group peer review to high standards, without immature criticisms or unhelpful praise.

Ongoing

Adjusting our performance depends on not only receiving feedback but also having opportunities to use it. What makes any assessment in education *formative* is not merely that it precedes summative assessments, but that the performer has opportunities, if results are less than optimal, to reshape the performance to better achieve the goal. In summative assessment, the feedback comes too late; the performance is over.

Thus, the more feedback I can receive in real time, the better my ultimate performance will be. This is how all highly successful computer games work. If you play Angry Birds, Halo, Guitar Hero, or Tetris, you know that the key to substantial improvement is that the feedback is both timely and ongoing. When you fail, you can immediately start over—sometimes even right where you left off—to get another opportunity to receive and learn from the feedback. (This powerful *feedback loop* is also user-friendly. Games are built to reflect and adapt to our changing need, pace, and ability to process information.)

It is telling, too, that performers are often judged on their ability to adjust in light of feedback. The ability to quickly adapt one's performance is a mark of all great achievers and problem solvers in a wide array of fields. Or, as many little league coaches say, "The problem is not making errors; you will all miss many balls in the field, and that's part of learning. The problem is when you don't learn from the errors."

Consistent

To be useful, feedback must be consistent. Clearly, performers can only adjust their performance successfully if the information fed back to them is stable, accurate, and trustworthy. In education, that means teachers have to be on the same page about what high-quality work is. Teachers need to look at student work together, becoming more consistent over time and formalizing their judgments in highly descriptive rubrics supported by anchor products and performances. By extension, if we want student-to-student feedback to be more helpful, students have to be trained to be consistent the same way we train teachers, using the same exemplars and rubrics.

Progress Toward a Goal

In light of these key characteristics of helpful feedback, how can schools most effectively use feedback as part of a system of formative assessment? The key is to gear feedback to long-term goals.

Let's look at how this works in sports. My daughter runs the mile in track. At the end of each lap in races and practice races, the coaches yell out *split times* (the times for each lap) and bits of feedback ("You're not swinging your arms!" "You're on pace for 5:15"), followed by advice ("Pick it up—you need to take two seconds off this next lap to get in under 5:10!").

My daughter and her teammates are getting feedback (and advice) about how they are performing now compared with their final desired time. My daughter's goal is to run a 5:00 mile. She has already run 5:09. Her coach is telling her that at the pace she just ran in the first lap, she is unlikely even to meet her best time so far this season, never mind her long-term goal. Then, he tells her something descriptive about her current performance (she's not swinging her arms) and gives her a brief piece of concrete advice (take two seconds off the next lap) to make achievement of the goal more likely.

The ability to improve one's result depends on the ability to adjust one's pace in light of ongoing feedback that measures performance against a concrete, long-term goal. But this isn't what most school district "pacing guides" and grades on "formative" tests tell you. They yield a grade against recent objectives taught, not useful feedback against the *final* performance standards. Instead of informing teachers and students at an interim date whether they are on track to achieve a desired level of student performance by the end of the school year, the guide and the test grade just provide a schedule for the teacher to follow in delivering content and a grade on that content. It's as if at the end of the first lap of the mile race, My daughter's coach simply yelled out, "*B+* on that lap!"

The advice for how to change this sad situation should be clear: Score student work in the fall and winter against spring standards, use more pre-and post-assessments to measure progress toward these standards, and do the item analysis to note what each student needs to work on for better future performance.

"But There's No Time!"

Although the universal teacher lament that there's no time for such feedback is understandable, remember that "no time to give and use feedback" actually means "no time to cause learning." As we have seen, research shows that *less* teaching plus *more* feedback is the key to achieving greater learning. And there are numerous ways—through technology, peers, and other teachers—that students can get the feedback they need.

So try it out. Less teaching, more feedback. Less feedback that comes only from you, and more tangible feedback designed into the performance itself.

References

Bransford, J. D., Brown, A. L., & Cocking, R. R. (Eds.). (2000). *How people learn: Brain, mind, experience, and school.* Washington, DC: National Academy Press.

Hattie, J. (2008). *Visible learning: A synthesis of over 800 meta-analyses relating to achievement.* New York: Routledge.

Marzano, R., Pickering, D., & Pollock, J. (2001). *Classroom instruction that works: Research-based strategies for increasing student achievement.* Alexandria, VA: ASCD.

Mazur, E. (2009, January 2). Farewell, lecture? *Science, 323,* 50–51.

Grant Wiggins was president of Authentic Education in Hopewell, New Jersey; www.authenticeducation.org. He was the author of *Educative Assessment: Designing Assessments to Inform and Improve Student Performance* (Jossey-Bass, 1998) and coauthor, with Jay McTighe, of many books in ASCD's Understanding by Design series.

Originally published in the September 2012 issue of *Educational Leadership, 70*(1): pp. 10–16.

Know Thy Impact

John Hattie

*Teachers give a lot of feedback, and not all of it is good. Here's how
to ensure you're giving students powerful feedback they can use.*

Many years ago, I made a claim about the importance of giving students
"dollops of feedback" (1999). This endorsement of giving great amounts
of feedback was based on the finding that feedback is among the most
powerful influences on how people learn.

The evidence comes from many sources. My synthesis of more
than 900 meta-analyses (2009, 2012) shows that feedback has one of
the highest effects on student learning. These meta-analyses focused
on many different influences on learning—home, school, teacher, and
curriculum—and were based on more than 50,000 individual studies,
comprising more than 200 million students, from 4- to 20-year-olds,
across all subjects. As an education researcher, I was seeking the
underlying story about what separated those influences that had
a greater effect on student learning from those that had a below-
average effect. Feedback was a common denominator in many of
the top influences. Moreover, Dylan Wiliam (2011) has argued that
feedback can double the rate of learning, and an increasing number of

scholars are researching this important notion (see Sutton, Hornsey, & Douglas, 2012).

I've come to regret my "dollops" claim because it ignores an important associated finding: The effects of feedback, although positive overall, are remarkably variable. There is as much ineffective as effective feedback. My work over the past years has concentrated on better understanding this variability and on clarifying what makes feedback effective—or not.

Some Questions to Start With

When we ask teachers and students what feedback looks and sounds like, we need to consider three important questions. The first question is, *Where is the student going?* Feedback that answers this question describes what success would look like in the area in which the student is working and what it would look like when he or she masters the current objective. Such feedback also tells us what the student would need to improve to get from here to there. For example, in a science class, the answer to, *Where am I going?* might be to "understand that light and sound are types of energy that are detected by ears and eyes"; students know they're there when they can discuss how light and sound enable people to communicate.

The second question is, *How is the student going?* Feedback that answers this question tells where the student is on the voyage of learning. What are the student's gaps, strengths, and current achievement? During the unit on light and sound, the teacher might give pop quizzes and encourage student questions and class discussion to show both students and teacher how they're going.

The third question—*Where to next?*—is particularly important. When we ask teachers to describe feedback, they typically reply that it's about constructive comments, criticisms, corrections, content, and elaboration. Students, however, value feedback that helps them know where they're supposed to go. The science teacher might point out, "Now that you understand types of energy, you can start to see how each affects our listening skills." If this *Where to next* part is missing, students are likely to ignore, misinterpret, or fail to act on the feedback they hear. They need to know where to put their effort and attention.

Of course, we want students to actively seek this feedback, but often a teacher's role is to provide resources, help, and direction when students don't know what to do. Simply put, students welcome feedback that is just in time, just for them, just for where they are in their learning process, and just what they need to move forward.

How to Make Feedback More Effective

For feedback to be effective, teachers need to clarify the goal of the lesson or activity, ensure that students understand the feedback, and seek feedback from students about the effectiveness of their instruction.

Clarify the Goal

The aim of feedback is to reduce the gap between where students are and where they should be. The teacher, therefore, needs to know what students bring to each lesson at the start and to articulate what success looks like. The teacher might demonstrate success with a worked example, scoring rubrics, demonstrations of steps toward a successful product, or progress charts. With a clear goal in mind, students are more likely to actively seek and listen to feedback.

A good comparison is to video games. The game keeps tabs on the player's prior learning (past performance); sets a challenge sufficiently above this prior learning to encourage the user to work out how to achieve the challenge; and provides many forms of feedback (positive and negative) to help the learner get to the target. The learner typically finds this process attractive enough to continue moving through increasingly challenging levels of the game.

In the same manner, effective teaching requires having a clear understanding of what each student brings to the lesson (his or her prior understanding, strategies for engaging in the lesson, and expectations of success); setting appropriate challenges that exceed this prior knowledge; and providing much feedback to assist the learner in moving from the prior to the desired set of understandings.

Ensure That Students Understand the Feedback

Teachers and leaders often *give* a lot of feedback, but much of this feedback isn't *received*. For example, when a teacher gives feedback to the whole class, many students think it's not meant for them but for someone else. Or sometimes we ask students to react a day later to feedback that a teacher has provided on an assignment. Students typically miss the teacher messages, don't understand them, or can't recall the salient points.

When we monitor how much academic feedback students actually receive in a typical class, it's a small amount indeed. Students hear the social, management, and behavior feedback, but they hear little feedback about tasks and strategies. Teachers would be far more effective if they could confirm whether students received and understood the feedback. This may mean listening to students outline how they interpret teachers' written comments on their work and what they intend to do next.

Seek Feedback from Students

When teachers enter their classrooms intending to seek and receive feedback from students about the effect of their teaching—both about their instruction, messages, and demands and about whether students need specific assistance, different strategies, or more or repetitions of particular information—the students are the major beneficiaries. These forms of feedback enable the teacher to adapt the flow of the lesson; to give needed directions or information to maximize students' chances of success; and to know whether it's necessary to reteach or offer different tasks, content, or strategies.

The Three Levels of Feedback

It's important to realize that feedback will look somewhat different at three separate levels:

Task Feedback

Feedback at this level describes how well the student performs a given task—such as distinguishing correct from incorrect answers, acquiring specific information, or building surface knowledge. The feedback clarifies what the student needs to do to improve his or her performance of that task.

For example, let's suppose a teacher is teaching students how to narrate events in a story in chronological order. The feedback to one student might be as follows:

> Your learning goal was to structure your account in a way that the first action you described was the first thing you did. Then you were to write about the other things you did in the same order in which they happened.
>
> You *did* write the first thing first—but after that it becomes muddled. You need to go through what you've written and number the order in which events happened and then rewrite them in that order.

Process Feedback

Feedback at this level describes the processes underlying or related to tasks, such as strategies students might use to detect or learn from errors, cues for seeking information, or ways to establish relationships among ideas.

For example, a teacher might suggest the following to a reader who stumbles on an unfamiliar word:

You're stuck on this word, and you've looked at me instead of trying to work it out. Can you see why you may have gotten it wrong? Perhaps you could sound out the word, look it up on your tablet, or infer its meaning from the other words in the paragraph.

Alternatively, a teacher might guide a student who is having difficulty relating ideas in a text by saying, "I've asked you to compare these ideas—for example, you could start out by listing ways they're similar or different. This would give you information about how they relate to one another."

Self-Regulation Feedback

This level of feedback describes how learners can monitor, direct, and regulate their own actions as they work toward the learning goal. Feedback at this level fosters the willingness and capability to seek and effectively deal with feedback, to self-assess and self-correct, to attribute success to effort more than to ability, and to develop effective help-seeking skills.

For example, when giving feedback to a proficient reader who is stumped by a vocabulary word, the teacher might say,

> I'm impressed you went back to the beginning of the sentence when you became stuck on this word. But in this case, this strategy didn't help. What else could you do? When you decide on what the word means, tell me how and why you know.

A teacher might promote a student's help-seeking and error-detection skills by saying the following:

> You checked your answer with the resource book and found you got it wrong. Any idea why you got it wrong? What strategy did you use? Can you think of a different strategy to try? How will you know if your answer is correct?

The power of feedback involves invoking the right level of feedback relative to whether the learner is a novice, somewhat proficient, or

competent. Novices mostly need task feedback; those who are somewhat proficient mostly need process feedback; and competent students
mostly need regulation or conceptual feedback.

In addition to maximizing feedback at the appropriate level,
teachers also need to be attentive to moving the student forward from
mastery of content to mastery of strategies to mastery of conceptual
understandings. For this to occur, teachers need to give students feedback that is *at and just above* their current level of learning.

Some Tips About What Works ...

Disconfirmation

Students may come to class with incorrect or poorly developed understandings of the topic being taught, and such misconceptions can
become a major barrier to learning. One of the more powerful forms
of feedback is listening to these notions and providing disconfirming
feedback. A teacher might say, "Let's assume what you said is correct
for the moment" and then work through an implication of the error.
Often such feedback is necessary to enable the student to go beyond
simply attaining factual knowledge to developing a deeper conceptual
understanding of the topic.

Formative Assessment

Because students often know how they'll do on a test, tests provide
students with little feedback information. However, if teachers create
and give assessments that aim to provide feedback about how they
taught, what they taught, and whom they taught well or poorly, that
information is powerful.

At the same time, teaching students how to receive such feedback
can help the students see what they know (their strengths) and don't
know (their gaps) and engage them more deeply in seeking feedback
or additional learning.

Instruction First

Feedback by itself rarely makes a difference because it doesn't occur in a vacuum. It needs to follow instruction. Teachers need to listen to the hum of student learning, welcoming quality student talk, structuring classroom discussions, inviting student questions, and openly discussing errors. If these reveal that students have misunderstood an important concept or failed to grasp the point of the lesson, sometimes the best approach is simply to reteach the material.

And Doesn't Work

Praise

The place of praise is an enigma in the feedback literature. Students welcome praise. Indeed, we all do. The problem is that when a teacher combines praise with other feedback information, the student typically only hears the praise. Evidence shows that praise can get in the way of students receiving feedback about the task and their performance (Skipper & Douglas, 2011). When a student hears "Good girl! But you should have paid attention to underlining the nouns," she certainly hears the first part loud and clear—but this can be the end of the feedback message.

Some claim that praise encourages effort and diligence, but the evidence is not strong (Kamins & Dweck, 1999). The bottom line seems to be this: Give much praise, but do *not* mix it with other feedback because praise dilutes the power of that information.

Peer Feedback

Noted education researcher Graham Nuthall (2007) placed microphones on students during the school day and then listened to their talk. One of his most crucial findings was that most of the feedback that students receive about their classroom work is from other students— and that much of this feedback is incorrect!

There's some evidence of the value of providing students with a rubric of the lesson flow to help them give more appropriate feedback to their peers on an assignment (see Hattie, 2012, p. 133). Such a rubric would show potential pathways a student might take (both correct and incorrect) at the task, process, and self-regulation levels. Through a series of questions—such as, What went wrong and why? or How can the student evaluate the information provided?—the rubric would guide feedback so it's more likely to help the student improve his or her performance.

Feedback for Life

Right now in my own work, I'm examining the mind frames that seem to underpin successful teaching and learning—and the most crucial is "Know thy impact." Gathering and assessing feedback are really the only ways teachers can know the impact of their teaching.

Some cautions here. First, feedback thrives in conditions of error or not knowing—not in environments where we already know and understand. Thus, teachers need to welcome error and misunderstanding in their classrooms. This attitude, of course, invokes trust. Students learn most easily in an environment in which they can get and use feedback about what they don't know without fearing negative reactions from their peers or their teacher.

Second, the simple act of giving feedback won't result in improved student learning—the feedback has to be effective. When teachers listen to their students' learning, they know what worked, what didn't, and what they need to change to foster student growth.

Using feedback isn't confined to a classroom. Consider its role in self-regulation and lifelong learning. We all stand to benefit from knowing when to seek feedback, how to seek it, and what to do with it when we get it.

References

Hattie, J. (1999). *Influences on student learning*. Inaugural professorial address, University of Auckland, New Zealand.

Hattie, J. (2009). *Visible learning: A synthesis of over 800 meta-analyses relating to achievement*. Oxford, UK: Routledge.

Hattie, J. (2012). *Visible learning for teachers: Maximizing impact on learning*. Oxford, UK: Routledge.

Kamins, M. L., & Dweck, C. S. (1999). Person versus process praise and criticism: Implications for contingent self-worth and coping. *Developmental Psychology, 35*(3), 835–847.

Nuthall, G. (2007). *The hidden lives of learners*. Wellington: New Zealand Council for Educational Research Press.

Skipper, Y., & Douglas, K. (2011). Is no praise good praise? Effects of positive feedback on children's and university students' responses to subsequent failures. *British Journal of Educational Psychology, 82*(2), 327–339.

Sutton, R., Hornsey, M. J., & Douglas, K. M. (Eds.). (2012). *Feedback: The communication of praise, criticism, and advice*. New York: Peter Lang.

Wiliam, D. (2011). *Embedded formative assessment*. Bloomington, IN: Solution Tree.

John Hattie (jhattie@unimelb.edu.au) is professor of education and director of the Melbourne Education Research Institute at the University of Melbourne, Australia. He is the author of *Visible Learning for Teachers: Maximizing Impact on Learning* (Routledge, 2012).

Originally published in the September 2012 issue of *Educational Leadership, 70*(1): pp. 18–23.

5

Feedback That Fits

Susan M. Brookhart

To craft teacher feedback that leads to learning,
put yourself in the student's shoes.

From the student's point of view, the ideal "script" for formative assessment reads something like, "Here is how close you are to the knowledge
or skills you are trying to develop, and here's what you need to do next."
The feedback teachers give students is at the heart of that script. But
feedback is only effective when it translates into a clear, positive message that students can hear.

Student Understanding and Control

The power of formative assessment lies in its double-barreled approach,
addressing both cognitive and motivational factors. Good formative
assessment gives students information they need to understand where
they are in their learning (the cognitive factor) and develops students'
feelings of control over their learning (the motivational factor).

Precisely because students' feelings of self-efficacy are involved,
however, even well-intentioned feedback can be very destructive if
the student reads the script in an unintended way ("See, I knew I was

stupid!"). Research on feedback shows its Jekyll-and-Hyde character. Not all studies of feedback show positive effects; the nature of the communication matters a great deal.

Recently, researchers have tried to tease out what makes some feedback effective, some ineffective, and some downright harmful (Butler & Winne, 1995; Hattie & Timperley, 2007; Kluger & DeNisi, 1996). Other researchers have described the characteristics of effective feedback (Johnston, 2004; Tunstall & Gipps, 1996). From parsing this research and reflecting on my own experience as an educational consultant working with elementary and secondary teachers on assessment issues, particularly the difference between formative assessment and grading, I have identified what makes for powerful feedback—in terms of how teachers deliver it and the content it contains.

Good feedback contains information a student can use. That means, first, that the student has to be able to hear and understand it. A student can't hear something that's beyond his comprehension, nor can a student hear something if she's not listening or if she feels like it's useless to listen. The most useful feedback focuses on the qualities of student work or the processes or strategies used to do the work. Feedback that draws students' attention to their self-regulation strategies or their abilities as learners is potent *if* students hear it in a way that makes them realize they will get results by expending effort and attention.

Following are suggestions for the most effective ways to deliver feedback and the most effective content of feedback. Notice that all these suggestions are based on knowing your students well. There is no magic bullet that will be just right for all students at all times.

Effective Ways to Deliver Feedback

When to Give Feedback

If a student is studying facts or simple concepts—like basic math—he or she needs immediate information about whether an answer is right or wrong—such as the kind of feedback flash cards give. For learning targets that develop over time, like writing or problem solving, wait until you have observed patterns in student work that provide insights into how they are doing the work, which will help you make suggestions about next steps. A general principle for gauging the timing of feedback is to put yourself in the student's place. When would a student want to hear feedback? When he or she is still thinking about the work, of course. It's also a good idea to give feedback as often as is practical, especially for major assignments.

How Much Feedback?

Probably the hardest decision concerns the *amount* of feedback. A natural inclination is to want to "fix" everything you see. That's the teacher's-eye view, where the target is perfect achievement of all learning goals. Try to see things from the student's-eye view. On which aspects of the learning target has the student done good work? Which aspects of the learning goals need improvement and should be addressed next? Are any assignments coming up that would make it wiser to emphasize one point over another? Consider also students' developmental level.

What Mode Is Best?

Some kinds of assignments lend themselves better to written feedback (for example, reviewing written work); some to oral feedback (observing as students do math problems); and some to demonstrations (helping a kindergarten student hold a pencil correctly). Some of the best feedback results from conversations *with* the student. Peter Johnston's (2004) book *Choice Words* discusses how to ask questions that help students help you provide feedback. For example, rather than telling the student all the things you notice about his or her work, start by asking, "What are you noticing about this? Does anything surprise you?" or "Why did you decide to do it this way?"

You should also decide whether individual or group feedback is best. Individual feedback tells a student that you value his or her learning, whereas group feedback provides opportunities for wider reteaching. These choices are not mutually exclusive. For example, say many students used bland or vague terms in a writing assignment. You might choose to give the whole class feedback on their word choices, with examples of how to use precise or vivid words, and follow up with thought-provoking questions for individual students, such as, "What other words could you use instead of *big*?" or "How could you describe this event so someone else would see how terrible it was for you?"

The Best Content for Feedback

Composing feedback is a skill in itself. The choices you make on *what* you say to a student will, of course, have a big influence on how the student interprets your feedback. Again, the main principle is considering the student's perspective.

Focus on Work and Process

Effective feedback describes the student's work, comments on the process the student used to do the work, and makes specific suggestions for what to do next. General praise ("Good job!") or personal comments don't help. The student might be pleased you approve, but not sure what was good about the work, and so unable to replicate its quality. Process-focused comments, on the other hand, give suggestions that move the work closer to the target, such as, "Can you rewrite that sentence so it goes better with the one before it?"

Relate Feedback to the Goal

For feedback to drive the formative assessment cycle, it needs to describe where the student is in relation to the learning goal. In so doing, it helps each student decide what his or her next goal should be. Feedback that helps a student see his or her own progress gives you a chance to point out the processes or methods that successful students use. ("I see you checked your work this time. Your computations were all correct, too! See how well that works?") Self-referenced feedback about the work itself ("Did you notice you have all the names capitalized this time?") is helpful for struggling students, who need to understand that they *can* make progress as much as they need to understand how far they are from the ultimate goal.

Try for Description, Not Judgment

Certain students are less likely to pay attention to descriptive feedback if it is accompanied by a formal judgment, like a grade or an evaluative comment. Some students will even hear judgment where you intend description. Unsuccessful learners have sometimes been so frustrated by their school experiences that they might see every attempt to help them as just another declaration that they are "stupid." For these learners, point out improvements over their previous performance, even if those improvements don't amount to overall success on the assignment. Then select one or two small, doable next steps. After the next round of work, give the student feedback on his or her success with those steps, and so on.

Be Positive and Specific

Being positive doesn't mean being artificially happy or saying work is good when it isn't. It means describing how the strengths in a student's work match the criteria for good work and how they show what that student is learning. And it means choosing words that communicate respect for the student and the work. Your tone should indicate that you are making helpful suggestions and giving the student a chance to take the initiative. ("This paper needs more detail. You could add more explanation about the benefits of recycling, or you could add more description of what should be done in your neighborhood. Which suggestion do you plan to try first?") If feedback comes across as a lecture or suggestions come across as orders, students will not understand that they are in charge of their own learning.

Feedback should be specific enough that the student knows what to do next, but not so specific that you do the work. Identifying errors or types of errors is a good idea, but correcting every error doesn't leave the student anything to do.

These feedback principles apply to both simple and complex assignments, and to all subjects and grade levels. The following example of ineffective and, especially, effective feedback on a writing assignment reflects these principles in practice.

A Tale of Two Feedback Choices

As part of a unit on how to write effective paragraphs, a 4th grade teacher assigned her students to write a paragraph answering the question, "Do dogs or cats make better pets?" They were asked to have a clear topic sentence, a clear concluding sentence, and at least three supporting details. Figure 5.1 shows what a student named Anna wrote and what *ineffective* teacher feedback on Anna's paragraph might look like.

To provide feedback, this teacher decided to make written comments on each student's paper and return the papers to students the day after they turned them in. So far, so good. However, the feedback in Figure 5.1 is all about the mechanics of writing. This doesn't match the learning target for this assignment, which was to structure a paragraph to make a point and to have that point contained in a topic sentence. Because the mechanical corrections are the only comments, the message seems to be that Anna's next step is to fix those errors. However, this teacher has already fixed the errors for her. All Anna has to do is recopy this paragraph. Moreover, there is no guarantee she would understand why some words and punctuation marks were changed. Recopying by rote could result in a "perfect" paragraph with no learning involved!

The worst part about this feedback, however, is that it doesn't communicate to Anna that she did, in fact, demonstrate the main paragraphing skills that were the learning target. Anna successfully

Figure 5.1: Ineffective Feedback on Anna's Writing Assignment

~~This is why~~ I like dogs better than cats. I think dogs are really playful. They can also be strong to pull you or something. They can come in different sizes like a Great Dane or a ~~Wener dog~~ Dachshund. They can also be in different colors. Some are just mutts. Others are pedigree. Best of all, dogs are cute and cuddly. That is why I like dogs a lot better than cats.

fashioned a topic sentence and a concluding sentence and provided supporting details. She needs to understand that she has accomplished this. Once she knows that, suggestions about how to make her good work even better make sense.

Figure 5.2 lists *effective* comments a teacher might write on Anna's paper or, preferably (because there is more to say than a teacher might want to write or a 4th grader might want to read), discuss with her in a brief conference. A teacher would probably use a few—but not all—of these comments, depending on circumstances.

Notice that these comments first compare the student's work with the criteria for the assignment, which were aligned with the learning goal. They acknowledge that Anna's paragraph shows that she understands how to produce a topic sentence, supporting details, and a concluding sentence.

The rest of the feedback choices depends on the context. How much time is available to discuss this paper? Which other feedback comments would align with learning targets that have previously been emphasized in class? Which of the possible next steps would be most beneficial for this particular student, given her previous writing? For example, if Anna is a successful writer who likes writing, she probably

Figure 5.2: Examples of Effective Feedback on Anna's Writing Assignment

Possible Teacher Comments	What's Best About This Feedback
Your topic sentence and concluding sentence are clear and go together well.	These comments describe achievement in terms of the criteria for the assignment. They show the student that you noticed these specific features and connected them to the criteria for good work.
You used a lot of details. I count seven different things you like about dogs.	
Your paragraph makes me wonder if you have a dog who is playful, strong, cute, and cuddly. Did you think about your own dog to write your paragraph? When you write about things you know, the writing often sounds real like this.	This comment would be especially useful for a student who had not previously been successful with the writing process. The comment identifies the strategy the student has used for writing and affirms that it was a good one. Note that "the writing often sounds genuine" might be better English, but "real" is probably clearer for this 4th grader.
Your reasons are all about dogs. Readers would already have to know what cats are like. They wouldn't know from your paragraph whether cats are playful, for instance. When you compare two things, write about both of the things you are comparing.	This constructive feedback criticizes a specific feature of the work, explains the reason for the criticism, and suggests what to do about it.
Did you check your spelling? See if you can find two misspelled words.	These comments about style and mechanics do not directly reflect the learning target, which was about paragraphing. However, they concern important writing skills. Their appropriateness would depend on how strongly spelling, style/usage, and word choice figure into the longer-term learning targets.
Feedback about making the topic sentence a stronger lead might best be done as a demonstration. In conference, show the student the topic sentence with and without "This is why" and ask which sentence she thinks reads more smoothly and why. Ask whether "This is why" adds anything that the sentence needs. You might point out that these words read better in the concluding sentence.	

already knows that describing traits she has observed in her own dog was a good strategy. If she has previously been an unsuccessful writer but has produced a paragraph better than her usual work—because the assignment finally asked a question about which she has something to say—it would be worth communicating to her that you noticed and naming "write about what you know" as a good strategy for future writing.

Feedback Practice Makes Perfect

Feedback choices present themselves continually in teaching. You have opportunities to give feedback as you observe students do their work in class and again as you look at the finished work. Take as many opportunities as you can to give students positive messages about how they are doing relative to the learning targets and what might be useful to do next. Make as many opportunities as you can to talk with your students about their work. As you do, you will develop a repertoire of feedback strategies that work for your subject area and students. The main thing to keep in mind when using any strategy is how students will hear, feel, and understand the feedback.

References

Butler, D. L., & Winne, P. H. (1995). Feedback and self-regulated learning: A theoretical synthesis. *Review of Educational Research, 65,* 245–281.

Hattie, J., & Timperley, H. (2007). The power of feedback. *Review of Educational Research, 77,* 81–112.

Johnston, P. H. (2004). *Choice words: How our language affects children's learning.* Portland, ME: Stenhouse.

Kluger, A. N., & DeNisi, A. (1996). The effects of feedback interventions on performance: A historical review, a meta-analysis, and a preliminary feedback intervention theory. *Psychological Bulletin, 119,* 254–284.

Tunstall, P., & Gipps, C. (1996). Teacher feedback to young children in formative assessment: A typology. *British Educational Research Journal, 22,* 389–404.

Susan M. Brookhart (susanbrookhart@bresnan.net) is an educational consultant and Senior Research Associate at the Center for Advancing the Study of Teaching and Learning (CASTL) at Duquesne University in Pittsburgh, Pennsylvania. She is the author of numerous ASCD titles, including the recent book, *How to Make Decisions with Different Types of Student Assessment Data* (ASCD, 2015).

Originally published in the December 2007/January 2008 issue of *Educational Leadership, 65*(4): pp. 54–59.

6

"How Am I Doing?"

Jan Chappuis

*Effective feedback helps students see what they know
and what they need to keep working on.*

One day when our daughter Claire was in 3rd grade, she brought home a math paper with a -3, a smiley face, and an *M* at the top. After we looked at it together, I asked, "What do you think this means you know?" She looked puzzled and said "Math." When I asked, "What do you think this means you need to learn?" she looked more puzzled and said, "Math?" Claire had no idea what the marks on her paper said about herself as a learner of mathematics. Her paper did not tell her what she was good at or what she needed to keep working on—the marks did not function as effective feedback.

We know that feedback plays a crucial role in bringing about learning gains. However, Lorrie Shepard (2001), in summarizing Kluger and De Nisi's meta-analysis on feedback research, points out that only in about one-third of the 131 studies examined did feedback improve learning.

It turns out that it isn't the *giving* of feedback that causes learning gains, it is the *acting* on feedback that determines how much students learn. Shepard and other researchers (Ames, 1992; Black & Wiliam, 1998; Butler, 1988; Hattie & Timperley, 2007) have concluded the following:

- *What* feedback describes is the key to its impact.
- Feedback that directs attention to the *intended learning* has a positive impact on achievement.
- Feedback is most effective when it points out strengths in the work and gives guidance for improvement.

Prerequisites for Effective Feedback

Unless students know the answer to the question, "Where am I going?", feedback is just a series of instructions disconnected from a learning destination. For example, as an elementary teacher I might have begun a lesson like this:

> OK kids, time for math. Remember, we're studying decimals. Take out your books and turn to page 152. Read the instructions at the top of page 152, and when you know what you're doing, send your table leader up to get your materials. We're going to go on a decimal hunt.

What have I told my students? The subject (mathematics); the topic (decimals); the resource (page 152 in the book); and the activity (decimal hunt). What have I not told them? The intended learning: "We are learning to read decimals and put decimal numbers in order." My students are on their own to figure out what they are learning. Chances are they think their job is to "go on a decimal hunt."

Absent a learning target, students will believe that the goal is to complete the activity. When students believe that *finishing* rather than *learning* is the goal of their effort, acting on feedback about place value may be regarded as more work, not an opportunity for learning.

Three conditions related to the learning need to be in place before we offer feedback. First, students need a clear vision of the intended learning. Second, our instructional activities need to align directly with the intended learning, and students need to see the connection between the learning and what they are doing. Third, assignments and assessments need to be set up so that students can interpret the results as indicators of what they have or have not yet learned.

Five Characteristics of Effective Feedback

Drawing from research, we can think of effective feedback as having five characteristics (Chappuis, 2009):

1. Effective feedback directs attention to the intended learning, pointing out strengths and offering specific information to guide improvement.

Effective feedback lets students know the strengths in their work and helps target problems to address. We can think of pointing out strengths as *success feedback*. For example, "The strongest part of your solution is ..." Success feedback can identify what the learner did correctly, describe a high-quality feature of the work, or point out the effective use of a strategy or process.

We can think of "guidance" as *intervention feedback*. For example, "The drawing you made didn't seem to help solve the problem. Try using the tree diagram we learned about yesterday." Intervention feedback generally identifies a correction, describes a feature needing work, points out a problem with a strategy or process, offers a reminder, makes a specific suggestion, or asks a question.

With younger students, we can use a form such as the "Stars and Stairs" shown in Figure 6.1, where the star is the success feedback and the stair is the intervention feedback. This helps establish a forward-looking stance to corrective feedback: "What's my next step? What do I need to do to accomplish this learning?"

Figure 6.1: Stars and Stairs Form

Teachers can use the Stars and Stairs form to provide feedback to younger students. The star indicates what the student is doing well, and the stair indicates steps the student needs to take to improve.

Name _____ Date _____

Source: Chappuis, Jan. *Seven strategies of assessment for learning* (1st ed., p. 208), © 2009. Reprinted by permission of Pearson Education, Inc., Upper Saddle River, NJ.

With older students, we can use a similar frame with a section labeled "That's Good" for success feedback and "Now This" for intervention feedback. If we want to monitor the actions students take, we can add a section to the form in which students note what they did with the feedback and identify one or more aspects that they think have really improved. (See www.ascd.org/el0912chappuis for an example form.) Their comments, which they turn in with the revised work, help us know whether they understand our feedback.

If the assessment information comes in the form of success criteria or a rubric, students can complete a form such as the one shown in Figure 6.2 *before* receiving feedback. We can then agree, offer additional information, or offer different information. Asking students to think about their work before receiving feedback scratches up the "soil" in

Figure 6.2: Assessment Dialogue Form

Students can complete the first part of this form before receiving feedback. The teacher then provides the feedback on the form, and the student responds with the plan for what to do next.

Name: _____ Date: _____

Assignment: _____

Feedback Focus: _____

MY OPINION

My strengths are _____

_____

What I think I need to work on is _____

_____

FEEDBACK

Strengths _____

_____

Work on _____

_____

MY PLAN

What I will do now _____

_____

_____

Source: Chappuis, Jan. *Seven strategies of assessment for learning* (1st ed., p. 80), © 2009. Reprinted by permission of Pearson Education, Inc., Upper Saddle River, NJ..

the brain so the feedback seeds have a place to settle in and grow. In addition, this protocol offers guided practice for students in becoming competent self-assessors.

2. Effective feedback occurs during the learning, while there is still time to act on it.

Sometimes we give feedback with a final mark or grade. For such feedback to influence subsequent learning, students must remember it, translate it into advice that is generalizable across tasks, and apply it the next time they encounter a task in which this learning could apply. Generally, strong students are able to do this, but struggling students aren't.

Think about a girls' volleyball coach. When the girls are practicing their serves, how long does the coach let them practice serving incorrectly? Vince Lombardi is frequently credited with saying, "Practice doesn't make perfect; practice makes *permanent.* Only *perfect* practice makes perfect." To ensure students are practicing perfectly, successful coaches intervene as soon as possible to correct errors in form or motion. They don't wait until after the game. In our classrooms, how long do we allow students to repeat a mistake or cement a misconception? "Where's the practice?" is the question that guides us to the most effective feedback point in the learning cycle.

3. Effective feedback addresses partial understanding.

When student work does not demonstrate at least partial understanding of a concept or process, feedback is not usually effective. In their 2007 meta-analysis of research on feedback, Hattie and Timperley conclude that when student work demonstrates little or no understanding the problems are best addressed through further instruction. Feedback can only build on learning; if the learning isn't there, the feedback isn't going to move it forward.

Corrective feedback in the absence of partial understanding can have a negative emotional effect (Hattie & Timperley, 2007). If students don't understand the task but try it anyway, and then receive feedback they don't understand, they can come to believe they are incapable of succeeding. One simple clue that a student's work is not ready for feedback is that you can't find any legitimate success feedback to offer. When the work doesn't demonstrate any understanding, don't give feedback—reteach instead.

4. Effective feedback does not do the thinking for the student.

If you have ever said to your child, "Clean up your room" more than once and then given in and cleaned it up yourself, the reason for this recommendation will be apparent. When I do the work for my child, I get a cleaner room, but my child is no closer to becoming a competent room cleaner. I haven't taught her to clean her room; I have taught her to wait me out.

When teachers provide students with more guidance than they need, feedback doesn't deepen the learning because students don't need to think. For example, teachers at the secondary level often notice that students' written work includes errors in conventions taught at earlier grades. Figure 6.3 shows three ways a teacher might give feedback on a sentence from a 10th grade social studies paper with typical errors. The first is an example of *overfeedbacking*, the equivalent of saying "clean up your room" and then doing the work yourself. The second example provides guidance by indicating which types of errors appear in each line (C = capitalization, U = usage, P = punctuation, S = spelling), but it doesn't do all of the student's thinking. The final example indicates areas still needing work, with a dot in the margin for each error in that line. The student is doing more of the thinking, thereby increasing the chances that he or she will learn from the experience.

5. Effective feedback limits corrective information to an amount the student can act on.

How much corrective feedback can each student reasonably be expected to act on in a given time? Information beyond that is less likely

Figure 6.3: Effective and Ineffective Feedback

These three examples show how a teacher might provide feedback on a sentence from a 10th grade social studies paper.

OverFeedback

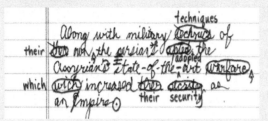

The feedback in the example above does the thinking for the student.

Feedback with Guidance

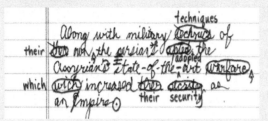

The feedback in the example above gives the student guidance on types of errors and where they appear (S = spelling, P = punctuation, C = capitalization).

Feedback That Notes Areas Needing Work

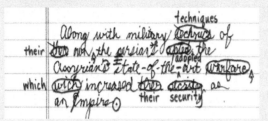

The feedback in the example above shows the student where errors appear but requires the student to determine what the errors are and how to correct them.

Source: Chappuis, Jan. *Seven strategies of assessment for learning* (1st ed., p. 80), © 2009. Reprinted by permission of Pearson Education, Inc., Upper Saddle River, NJ..

to be used. In a review of research on written composition, George Hillocks (1986) noted that in studies on error correcting, teachers who marked every error were no more effective in increasing the quality of students' work than teachers who only marked the errors that current instruction focused on.

Students differ in their capacity for responding to correction, and too much corrective feedback at one time can cause a student to shut down, guaranteeing that no further learning will take place. In such cases, consider letting go of the urge to provide all correctives necessary to make the work perfect and instead provide as much guidance as the student can reasonably act on.

Feedback Leading to Action

Recently, I accompanied my mother to doctors' appointments in preparation for a difficult surgery. She interacted positively in some situations and negatively in others, and she walked out of one appointment. When I asked her about the differences, she told me she trusts the doctors and nurses who listen to her and doesn't trust the ones who don't. Regardless of what treatment is in her best interest, she only wants to take the advice of the ones she trusts because they took information in before giving advice out.

There is a lesson here for educators. For feedback to be effective, students must act on it, and we can enhance our students' willingness to act on our feedback. By looking closely at their work to understand what they understand and identify where they need help, we are listening to our students. Our feedback can communicate to them that we have heard them, and they will be more likely to trust us enough to follow our advice for that sometimes-difficult next step.

References

Ames, C. (1992). Classrooms: Goals, structures, and student motivation. *Journal of Educational Psychology, 84*(3), 261–271.

Black, P., & Wiliam, D. (1998). Assessment and classroom learning. *Assessment in Education, 5*(1), 7–74.

Butler, R. (1988). Enhancing and undermining intrinsic motivation: The effects of task-involving and ego-involving evaluation on interest and performance. *British Journal of Educational Psychology, 58*, 1–14.

Chappuis, J. (2009). *Seven strategies of assessment for learning.* Upper Saddle River, NJ: Pearson Education.

Hattie, J., & Timperley, H. (2007). The power of feedback. *Review of Educational Research, 77*(1), 81–112.

Hillocks, G. (1986). *Research on written composition: New directions for teaching.* Fairfax, VA: National Council of Teachers of English. (ERIC Document Retrieval Service No. ED265552)

Shepard, L. A. (2001). The role of classroom assessment in teaching and learning. In V. Richardson (Ed.), *Handbook of research on teaching* (4th ed., pp. 1066–1101). Washington, DC: American Educational Research Association.

Jan Chappius (Jan.Chappuis@Pearson.com) is vice president of Pearson Assessment Training Institute in Portland, Oregon.

Originally published in the September 2012 issue of *Educational Leadership, 70*(1): pp. 36–41.

7

The Perils and Promises of Praise

Carol S. Dweck

The wrong kind of praise creates self-defeating behavior.
The right kind motivates students to learn.

We often hear these days that we've produced a generation of young people who can't get through the day without an award. They expect success because they're special, not because they've worked hard.

Is this true? Have we inadvertently done something to hold back our students?

I think educators commonly hold two beliefs that do just that. Many believe that (1) praising students' intelligence builds their confidence and motivation to learn, and (2) students' inherent intelligence is the major cause of their achievement in school. Our research has shown that the first belief is false and that the second can be harmful—even for the most competent students.

As a psychologist, I have studied student motivation for more than 35 years. My graduate students and I have looked at thousands of children, asking why some enjoy learning, even when it's hard, and why they are resilient in the face of obstacles. We have learned a great deal. Research shows us how to praise students in ways that yield motivation and resilience. In addition, specific interventions can reverse a student's slide into failure during the vulnerable period of adolescence.

Fixed or Malleable?

Praise is intricately connected to how students view their intelligence. Some students believe that their intellectual ability is a fixed trait. They have a certain amount of intelligence, and that's that. Students with this fixed mind-set become excessively concerned with how smart they are, seeking tasks that will prove their intelligence and avoiding ones that might not (Dweck, 1999, 2006). The desire to learn takes a backseat.

Other students believe that their intellectual ability is something they can develop through effort and education. They don't necessarily believe that anyone can become an Einstein or a Mozart, but they do understand that even Einstein and Mozart had to put in years of effort to become who they were. When students believe that they can develop their intelligence, they focus on doing just that. Not worrying about how smart they will appear, they take on challenges and stick to them (Dweck, 1999, 2006).

More and more research in psychology and neuroscience supports the growth mind-set. We are discovering that the brain has more plasticity over time than we ever imagined (Doidge, 2007); that fundamental aspects of intelligence can be enhanced through learning (Sternberg, 2005); and that dedication and persistence in the face of obstacles are key ingredients in outstanding achievement (Ericsson, Charness, Feltovich, & Hoffman, 2006).

Alfred Binet (1909/1973), the inventor of the IQ test, had a strong growth mind-set. He believed that education could transform the basic capacity to learn. Far from intending to measure fixed intelligence, he meant his test to be a tool for identifying students who were not profiting from the public school curriculum so that other courses of study could be devised to foster their intellectual growth.

The Two Faces of Effort

The fixed and growth mind-sets create two different psychological worlds. In the fixed mind-set, students care first and foremost about how they'll be judged: smart or not smart. Repeatedly, students with this mind-set reject opportunities to learn if they might make mistakes (Hong, Chiu, Dweck, Lin, & Wan, 1999; Mueller & Dweck, 1998). When they do make mistakes or reveal deficiencies, rather than correct them, they try to hide them (Nussbaum & Dweck, 2007).

They are also afraid of effort because effort makes them feel dumb. They believe that if you have the ability, you shouldn't need effort (Blackwell, Trzesniewski, & Dweck, 2007), that ability should bring success all by itself. This is one of the worst beliefs that students can hold. It can cause many bright students to stop working in school when the curriculum becomes challenging.

Finally, students in the fixed mind-set don't recover well from setbacks. When they hit a setback in school, they *decrease* their efforts and consider cheating (Blackwell et al., 2007). The idea of fixed intelligence does not offer them viable ways to improve.

Let's get inside the head of a student with a fixed mind-set as he sits in his classroom, confronted with algebra for the first time. Up until then, he has breezed through math. Even when he barely paid attention in class and skimped on his homework, he always got As. But this is different. It's hard. The student feels anxious and thinks, "What if I'm not as good at math as I thought? What if other kids understand it and I don't?" At some level, he realizes that he has two choices: try hard, or turn off. His interest in math begins to wane, and his attention wanders. He tells himself, "Who cares about this stuff? It's for nerds. I could do it if I wanted to, but it's so boring. You don't see CEOs and sports stars solving for x and y."

By contrast, in the growth mind-set, students care about learning. When they make a mistake or exhibit a deficiency, they correct it (Blackwell et al., 2007; Nussbaum & Dweck, 2007). For them, effort is a *positive* thing: It ignites their intelligence and causes it to grow. In the face of failure, these students escalate their efforts and look for new learning strategies.

Let's look at another student—one who has a growth mind-set—having her first encounter with algebra. She finds it new, hard, and confusing, unlike anything else she has ever learned. But she's determined to understand it. She listens to everything the teacher says, asks the teacher questions after class, and takes her textbook home and reads the chapter over twice. As she begins to get it, she feels exhilarated. A new world of math opens up for her.

It is not surprising, then, that when we have followed students over challenging school transitions or courses, we find that those with growth mind-sets outperform their classmates with fixed mind-sets—even when they entered with equal skills and knowledge. A growth mind-set fosters the growth of ability over time (Blackwell et al., 2007; Mangels, Butterfield, Lamb, Good, & Dweck, 2006; see also Grant & Dweck, 2003).

The Effects of Praise

Many educators have hoped to maximize students' confidence in their abilities, their enjoyment of learning, and their ability to thrive in school by praising their intelligence. We've studied the effects of this kind of praise in children as young as 4 years old and as old as adolescence, in students in inner-city and rural settings, and in students of different ethnicities—and we've consistently found the same thing (Cimpian, Arce, Markman, & Dweck, 2007; Kamins & Dweck, 1999; Mueller & Dweck, 1998): Praising students' intelligence gives them a short burst of pride, followed by a long string of negative consequences.

In many of our studies (see Mueller & Dweck, 1998), 5th grade students worked on a task, and after the first set of problems, the teacher praised some of them for their intelligence ("You must be smart at these problems") and others for their effort ("You must have worked hard at these problems"). We then assessed the students' mind-sets. In one study, we asked students to agree or disagree with mind-set statements, such as, "Your intelligence is something basic about you that you can't really change." Students praised for intelligence agreed with statements like these more than students praised for effort did. In another study, we asked students to define intelligence. Students praised for intelligence made significantly more references to innate, fixed capacity, whereas the students praised for effort made more references to skills, knowledge, and areas they could change through effort and learning. Thus, we found that praise for intelligence tended to put students in a fixed mind-set (intelligence is fixed, and you have it), whereas praise for effort tended to put them in a growth mind-set (you're developing these skills because you're working hard).

We then offered students a chance to work on either a challenging task that they could learn from or an easy one that ensured error-free performance. Most of those praised for intelligence wanted the easy task, whereas most of those praised for effort wanted the challenging task and the opportunity to learn.

Next, the students worked on some challenging problems. As a group, students who had been praised for their intelligence *lost* their confidence in their ability and their enjoyment of the task as soon as they began to struggle with the problem. If success meant they were smart, then struggling meant they were not. The whole point of intelligence praise is to boost confidence and motivation, but both were gone in a flash. Only the effort-praised kids remained, on the whole, confident and eager.

When the problems were made somewhat easier again, students praised for intelligence did poorly, having lost their confidence and motivation. As a group, they did worse than they had done initially on these same types of problems. The students praised for effort showed excellent performance and continued to improve.

Finally, when asked to report their scores (anonymously), almost 40 percent of the intelligence-praised students lied. Apparently, their egos were so wrapped up in their performance that they couldn't admit mistakes. Only about 10 percent of the effort-praised students saw fit to falsify their results.

Praising students for their intelligence, then, hands them not motivation and resilience but a fixed mind-set with all its vulnerability. In contrast, effort or "process" praise (praise for engagement, perseverance, strategies, improvement, and the like) fosters hardy motivation. It tells students what they've done to be successful and what they need to do to be successful again in the future. Process praise sounds like this:

- You really studied for your English test, and your improvement shows it. You read the material over several times, outlined it, and tested yourself on it. That really worked!
- I like the way you tried all kinds of strategies on that math problem until you finally got it.
- It was a long, hard assignment, but you stuck to it and got it done. You stayed at your desk, kept up your concentration, and kept working. That's great!
- I like that you took on that challenging project for your science class. It will take a lot of work—doing the research, designing the machine, buying the parts, and building it. You're going to learn a lot of great things.

What about a student who gets an *A* without trying? I would say, "All right, that was too easy for you. Let's do something more challenging that you can learn from." We don't want to make something done quickly and easily the basis for our admiration.

What about a student who works hard and *doesn't* do well? I would say, "I liked the effort you put in. Let's work together some more and figure out what you don't understand." Process praise keeps students focused, not on something called ability that they may or may not have and that magically creates success or failure, but on processes they can all engage in to learn.

Motivated to Learn

Finding that a growth mind-set creates motivation and resilience—and leads to higher achievement—we sought to develop an intervention that would teach this mind-set to students. We decided to aim our intervention at students who were making the transition to 7th grade because this is a time of great vulnerability. School often gets more difficult in 7th grade, grading becomes more stringent, and the environment becomes more impersonal. Many students take stock of themselves and their intellectual abilities at this time and decide whether they want to be involved with school. Not surprisingly, it is often a time of disengagement and plunging achievement.

We performed our intervention in a New York City junior high school in which many students were struggling with the transition and were showing plummeting grades. If students learned a growth mind-set, we reasoned, they might be able to meet this challenge with increased, rather than decreased, effort. We therefore developed an eight-session workshop in which both the control group and the growth-mind-set group learned study skills, time management techniques, and memory strategies (Blackwell et al., 2007). However, in the growth-mind-set intervention, students also learned about their brains and what they could do to make their intelligence grow.

They learned that the brain is like a muscle—the more they exercise it, the stronger it becomes. They learned that every time they try hard and learn something new, their brain forms new connections that, over time, make them smarter. They learned that intellectual development is not the natural unfolding of intelligence, but rather the formation of new connections brought about through effort and learning.

Students were riveted by this information. The idea that their intellectual growth was largely in their hands fascinated them. In fact, even the most disruptive students suddenly sat still and took notice, with the most unruly boy of the lot looking up at us and saying, "You mean I don't have to be dumb?"

Indeed, the growth-mind-set message appeared to unleash students' motivation. Although both groups had experienced a steep decline in their math grades during their first months of junior high, those receiving the growth-mind-set intervention showed a significant rebound. Their math grades improved. Those in the control group, despite their excellent study skills intervention, continued their decline.

What's more, the teachers—who were unaware that the intervention workshops differed—singled out three times as many students in the growth-mindset intervention as showing marked changes in motivation. These students had a heightened desire to work hard and learn. One striking example was the boy who thought he was dumb. Before this experience, he had never put in any extra effort and often didn't turn his homework in on time. As a result of the training, he worked for hours one evening to finish an assignment early so that his teacher could review it and give him a chance to revise it. He earned a *B+* on the assignment (he had been getting *C*s and lower previously).

Other researchers have obtained similar findings with a growth-mind-set intervention. Working with junior high school students, Good, Aronson, and Inzlicht (2003) found an increase in math and English achievement test scores; working with college students, Aronson, Fried, and Good (2002) found an increase in students' valuing of academics, their enjoyment of schoolwork, and their grade point averages.

To facilitate delivery of the growth-mind-set workshop to students, we developed an interactive computer-based version of the intervention called *Brainology.* Students work through six modules, learning about the brain, visiting virtual brain labs, doing virtual brain experiments, seeing how the brain changes with learning, and learning how they can make their brains work better and grow smarter.

We tested our initial version in 20 New York City schools, with encouraging results. Almost all students (anonymously polled) reported changes in their study habits and motivation to learn resulting directly from their learning of the growth mind-set. One student noted that as a result of the animation she had seen about the brain, she could actually "picture the neurons growing bigger as they make more connections." One student referred to the value of effort: "If you do not give up and you keep studying, you can find your way through."

Adolescents often see school as a place where they perform for teachers who then judge them. The growth mind-set changes that perspective and makes school a place where students vigorously engage in learning for their own benefit.

Going Forward

Our research shows that educators cannot hand students confidence on a silver platter by praising their intelligence. Instead, we can help them gain the tools they need to maintain their confidence in learning by keeping them focused on the *process* of achievement.

Maybe we have produced a generation of students who are more dependent, fragile, and entitled than previous generations. If so, it's time for us to adopt a growth mind-set and learn from our mistakes. It's time to deliver interventions that will truly boost students' motivation, resilience, and learning.

References

Aronson, J., Fried, C., & Good, C. (2002). Reducing the effects of stereotype threat on African American college students by shaping theories of intelligence. *Journal of Experimental Social Psychology, 38*, 113–125.

Binet, A. (1909/1973). *Les idées modernes sur les enfants* [Modern ideas on children]. Paris: Flamarion. (Original work published 1909)

Blackwell, L., Trzesniewski, K., & Dweck, C. S. (2007). Implicit theories of intelligence predict achievement across an adolescent transition: A longitudinal study and an intervention. *Child Development, 78*, 246–263.

Cimpian, A., Arce, H., Markman, E. M., & Dweck, C. S. (2007). Subtle linguistic cues impact children's motivation. *Psychological Science, 18*, 314–316.

Doidge, N. (2007). *The brain that changes itself: Stories of personal triumph from the frontiers of brain science*. New York: Viking.

Dweck, C. S. (1999). *Self-theories: Their role in motivation, personality and development*. Philadelphia: Taylor and Francis/Psychology Press.

Dweck, C. S. (2006). *Mindset: The new psychology of success*. New York: Random House.

Ericsson, K. A., Charness, N., Feltovich, P. J., & Hoffman, R. R. (Eds.). (2006). *The Cambridge handbook of expertise and expert performance*. New York: Cambridge University Press.

Good, C., Aronson, J., & Inzlicht, M. (2003). Improving adolescents' standardized test performance: An intervention to reduce the effects of stereotype threat. *Journal of Applied Developmental Psychology, 24*, 645–662.

Grant, H., & Dweck, C. S. (2003). Clarifying achievement goals and their impact. *Journal of Personality and Social Psychology, 85*, 541–553.

Hong, Y. Y., Chiu, C., Dweck, C. S., Lin, D., & Wan, W. (1999). Implicit theories, attributions, and coping: A meaning system approach. *Journal of Personality and Social Psychology, 77*, 588–599.

Kamins, M., & Dweck, C. S. (1999). Person vs. process praise and criticism: Implications for contingent self-worth and coping. *Developmental Psychology, 35*, 835–847.

Mangels, J. A., Butterfield, B., Lamb, J., Good, C. D., & Dweck, C. S. (2006). Why do beliefs about intelligence influence learning success? A social-cognitive-neuroscience model. *Social, Cognitive, and Affective Neuroscience, 1*, 75–86.

Mueller, C. M., & Dweck, C. S. (1998). Intelligence praise can undermine motivation and performance. *Journal of Personality and Social Psychology, 75*, 33–52.

Nussbaum, A. D., & Dweck, C. S. (2007). Defensiveness vs. remediation: Self-theories and modes of self-esteem maintenance. *Personality and Social Psychology Bulletin.*

Sternberg, R. (2005). Intelligence, competence, and expertise. In A. Elliot & C. S. Dweck (Eds.), *The handbook of competence and motivation* (pp. 15–30). New York: Guilford Press.

Carol S. Dweck is the Lewis and Virginia Eaton Professor of Psychology at Stanford University and the author of *Mindset: The New Psychology of Success* (Random House, 2006).

Originally published in the October 2007 issue of *Educational Leadership, 65*(2): pp. 34–39.

8

Formative Assessment in Seven Good Moves

Brent Duckor

By listening carefully to what students say and thinking deeply about how to better guide them, teachers can become accomplished formative assessors.

The research is clear: What teachers do in their classrooms matters. But which practices really make a difference? John Hattie (2012) conducted an extensive meta-analysis, looking at 800 meta-analyses that focused on locating a specific student achievement outcome and identifying an influence on that outcome. Formative assessment topped his list of the most influential practices that improve student outcomes.

What makes formative assessment so effective? It depends on whom you talk to. Although experts tell us that formative assessment is one of the most powerful ways to raise student achievement (Black & Wiliam, 1998), we don't always know *which* practices are most effective, *when* to deploy them, and *why* a particular combination actually worked for a particular student in a particular classroom. We often hear that the best feedback practices must be specific, addressable, timely, ongoing, and content-rich (Wiggins, 2012). But many beginning teachers and administrators don't have a clear idea of what these terms mean.

For informed teacher educators, formative assessment is more than a checklist of qualities or collection of activities. Rather, it's made up of a sequence of moves that invite a positive, ongoing relationship between teachers and their students. It's the job of teacher educators to connect theory to practice and work with beginners to become better formative assessors.

Seven Essential Moves

Through watching hours of videotaped lessons and observing even more live lessons in middle and high school classrooms, my colleagues and I have identified seven basic moves that are essential to rich formative assessment practice (Duckor, Honda, Pink, Wilmot, & Wilson, 2012). These moves involve asking effective questions, giving students adequate time to think and respond, and asking probing follow-up questions that deepen student understanding. By practicing these moves, beginning teachers can develop into skillful assessors.

We created the names for these seven formative assessment moves to better describe to teacher candidates what we, as teacher educators, are looking for during observations in the classroom.

Move 1. Prime students first.

Priming sets the stage for all other formative assessment moves. Teachers will need to let the class know they'll be asking questions and calling on students in ways that students may be unfamiliar with. Questions will also prompt students to more deeply reflect on their classmates' responses and make new connections. Some students may experience this new classroom culture as strange.

For example, if a teacher follows up on a student's response by asking, "Can you say more about why that is?" some students might see this as a challenge or even a personal attack. A more positive follow-up question—such as, "I like this idea. Could you elaborate, explaining it in your own words?"—would more likely encourage a fuller and richer student response.

Thus, teachers need to establish norms and routines for inviting student participation, especially for students who aren't familiar with assessment practices outside the normal experience of "doing school." They also need to reflect on the various moves they do implement, whether it's increasing wait time or not having students raise hands to answer questions. By keeping notes on how the various approaches worked and with which students, we can agree on goals for the beginning teacher's next steps in becoming a more competent formative assessor (Duckor & Holmberg, 2013).

Like anthropologists doing fieldwork, teachers who are developing their skills in formative assessment are trying to understand and practice a new way of school life—for themselves and for their students. In the formative assessment–driven classroom, everyone is consciously engaged in practices that promote further learning, as opposed to those that merely assess student achievement (Stiggins, 2002).

It's not uncommon for students who have suddenly been immersed in this "foreign" classroom culture to ask questions like these:

- Why is the teacher asking "why?" so much?
- Why is the teacher using equity sticks (Popsicle sticks with a student's name written on each one) to call on us?
- Why is the teacher waiting a bit before taking answers, instead of just calling on Mary and John, who have their hands up?
- Why is the teacher putting *all* answers on the whiteboard, even the wrong ones?
- Why is the teacher always answering a question with another question?
- Why can't the teacher just solve the problem and write the correct answer on the board so we can move on?

Unfortunately, the literature on formative assessment provides few accounts of the culture shock many students experience when they're expected to learn in this new and perhaps puzzling manner.

Move 2. Pose good questions.

Asking questions seems so easy. Teachers prompt students here and there to answer a few questions during a lecture, typically calling on just a few students to give the correct answer. Most students simply nod their heads while waiting for the teacher to get back to the lecture.

When it comes to effective posing of questions, the *kinds* of questions teachers ask matter. In the beginning teacher's classroom, questions often fall flat. Sometimes the questions imply a right/wrong dichotomy, which fails to invite or elicit a range of student responses. For example, "Can someone give me the definition of mitosis?"

Other times, the questions are too open-ended. They tend to overshoot and intimidate students: "Why did the French Revolution occur?" "How do polynomial functions work?" "Can someone tell me what a thesis is?"

But some questions can promote thinking and learning. An effective question sizes up the context for learning, has a purpose related to the lesson and unit plan, and, ideally, is related to larger essential questions in the discipline. During a lesson on the civil rights movement (Gold & Lanzoni, 1993), a teacher at New York's Central Park East Secondary School asked students, "Should the integration of public facilities [in this scenario, a skating rink owned by whites] extend beyond the ruling on education addressed by the *Brown v. Board of Education* decision?" As the students worked to integrate primary sources into their oral arguments—and used words from those documents to make sense of such concepts as segregation, integration, and equality—they engaged in a lively give-and-take discussion. All the while, the teacher pushed back on their diverse responses, inviting deeper reflection.

Posing good questions requires that teachers *know their audience* and adapt questioning strategies to the responses of their students in real time. A well-posed question creates an opportunity to meet learners at their current level of understanding. Thus, formative assessors need to know (or at least anticipate) their students' learning progressions with complex material so they can scaffold questions at key points (pit stops and bottlenecks) in the unit.

Move 3. Pause during questioning.

We all need time to process information, to "transfer files" from our short-term to our long-term memory and back again. Our processing speed varies according to the nature of the information we're asked to process and our degree of familiarity with it. That said, beginning teachers tend to feel uncomfortable with wait time between their questions and their students' responses. Moreover, they don't provide their students with enough protocols for participation, such as turn-and-talk, think-pair-share, or polling for opinions, all of which can provide the wait time needed to increase participation.

Pausing requires preparation. A stopwatch, a smartphone, or a variety of audio or video devices can help track time between a question and a response. Teachers might also try counting out the pause in their heads. The goal is to slow the process down.

One low-tech solution to slowing down the question-and-answer exchange is to set up a think-pair-share and journal entry routine after posing a question to the class. Students can briefly talk to one another, then write out their responses in their journals, and then raise their hands to show they're ready to address the teacher's question.

In a heterogeneous classroom with language learners, students with special needs, and students with different learning styles, pausing can make all the difference. Giving students extra time to clarify their thinking gets more students into the discussion and makes teachers more aware of the level of understanding of every student in the class.

In the absence of such information, the formative assessor doesn't even know where to start with follow-up questioning strategies designed to further elicit student thinking.

Move 4. Probe student responses.

Too often, beginning teachers ask a question as though the answer to that question were obvious: "Does everyone understand?" "Did you copy the information yet?" "Can we move on now?" Or the teacher will ask a question that has a single right answer. As soon as one student answers the question correctly, there's no need for follow-up because "we" now have the correct answer. Compounding the difficulty, teachers may pose a question, get a correct response, and then silently wonder, "OK, now what do I do?" Thus the familiar, "Uh … good job!"

Probing suggests there's always more to know. Asking the standard questions (Who? What? Where? When? How? Why?) may lead to an initial set of student responses that satisfy the requirement for getting through the lesson in time for Friday's quiz. But formative assessment is more than a march toward the known. It's a process for uncovering deeper understanding, which means having access to evidence about what students are thinking.

For example, how can a teacher know whether a student truly understands why things sink or float without first posing the question and then probing a variety of possible responses? Research on buoyancy misconceptions reveals that students typically think that big, heavy things sink and small, light things float; that hollow things float; and that sharp edges make things sink (Yin, Tomita, & Shavelson, 2008). After asking students why some things float and others sink, the teacher might ask, "So who thinks things float because they're hollow? Can you say why? Turn to your partner and ask for an example of a hollow thing that might sink."

Probing is about collecting more substantial evidence to make decisions about what to teach, reteach, or even preteach for a particular group of students. The more one learns about how real students in a particular classroom approach the material, the better one can guide them through the bottlenecks, cul-de-sacs, and eddies that will inevitably mark a student's progression toward an understanding of conceptually difficult material.

Move 5. Bounce questions throughout the classroom.

Feedback is about generating a loop. That loop can be represented by the connections or nodes of talk in the classroom. Too often, the loop is too small, occurring mostly between the teacher and a few eager students.

Beginning teachers often pounce on the first hand raised in response to a question. There seems to be an unbreakable bond between teachers who struggle to elicit the correct answer from their students and the small number of willing students who have that answer. Too often, the symbiotic relationship between these two or three students and the teacher leads to a false sense of feedback. When asked after a lesson, "So who seems to understand the objective of the lesson?" the beginning teacher typically recalls the answers that the hardworking, engaged students supplied.

Teachers can use equity sticks, index cards, or other tools to generate a "bounce" of responses across the classroom. They can even make notations on the seating chart to keep track of patterns of participation. By increasing the breadth and depth of student responses, the teacher is better able to draw meaningful conclusions about student understanding.

Without consistent procedures and visible practices related to "bouncing," or spreading questions throughout the classroom, there's little hope that the majority of the students will actually engage in thinking through a topic. We know from research on academic language and English language development that providing opportunities for students to articulate their thinking—in a variety of productive modes—is essential. This practice also makes it more likely that all students will feel included in classroom conversations (Zwiers, 2007).

Move 6. Use tagging to generate a wide range of responses.

A biology teacher begins class by writing the word *cell* on the whiteboard and asking, "What is a cell?" Several students shout out their answers. The teacher says, "Not quite, but good tries"; writes the correct textbook definition on the whiteboard; and asks students to copy it into their journals. Bad move.

Tagging is recognizing student contributions to questions posed by the teacher (or other students). A simple tagging routine is the word web. Experienced formative assessors put a word up in the classroom, making it visible to all students—for example, "What is the first thing that pops into your head when you see the word *ratio*?" Then they ask students to write down their thinking. The word webs that emerge from these call-and-response brainstorming procedures encompass both on- and off-target responses, which all build a better picture of student thinking about the topic.

Sometimes it helps to have students turn to a peer and share a response or question orally before they write. Students might write a definition or draw a picture—whatever works to get their thinking started. The idea is to generate a wide range of responses.

Researchers point out that teachers are often uncomfortable with soliciting unorthodox or wrong answers (Black & Wiliam, 1998). Teachers may think that misconceptions could derail the discussion. Of course, misconceptions and students' prior knowledge are at the very heart of the learning process in a formative assessment–driven classroom (Shepard, 2000). If teachers don't create a space for students to express both their understandings and their misunderstandings, students who are too embarrassed to express a potentially incorrect answer will simply remain silent.

Move 7. Build your bins.

We come full circle with the seventh move, binning. If posing questions is the alpha, then binning is the omega move for the skilled formative assessor. Bins are how we teachers categorize student responses. We label some bins *correct answer*, others *misconception*, others *proficient*, and so on. Educational psychologists might refer to bins as mental schema for assimilating and accommodating new experiences. When students respond to a question, the teacher can potentially categorize, sort, and "bin" it for later use.

For example, beginning teachers often have difficulty hearing any responses that don't fall into their *correct answer* bin. They're often unfamiliar with student learning progressions—how students work themselves through the building blocks of a big idea. In the science curriculum that deals with why things sink or float, for example, teachers should know about common student misconceptions related to mass, volume, density, and relative density. By failing to tag responses that evoke those misconceptions, teachers reduce the power of formative assessment to uncover difficult learning steps along the way. A teacher needs to know, through practical training and rich classroom experience, where kids get stuck and why.

How to build this teacher knowledge of different students' learning progressions, in relation to different topics and different levels of background knowledge, is one of the most important formative assessment challenges (Heritage, 2008).

Practice, Practice, Practice: On Making Good Moves

Our challenge as teacher educators is to plant the seeds of formative assessment in our preservice teachers so those seeds take root and flourish in these teachers' careers. Of course, beginning teachers are overwhelmed by many demands—classroom management, content-knowledge preparation, grading, and staying on top of their workloads, to name a few. Beginning teachers may also feel constrained by conflicting messages about what matters to students, parents, and administrators.

However, because formative assessment has such a great effect on student outcomes, beginning teachers need to take note. By practicing these seven basic moves, all teachers can develop the requisite expertise and become more skilled formative assessors. Research shows us that formative assessment makes a difference not only for student outcomes, but also for principals and teachers looking to build stronger relationships in their schools and classrooms.

References

Black, P., & Wiliam, D. (1998). Inside the black box: Raising standards through classroom assessment. *Phi Delta Kappan, 80*(2), 139–148.

Duckor, B., & Holmberg, C. (2013). Helping beginning student teachers uncover the art and science of formative feedback. *California English, 18*(4), 8–10.

Duckor, B., Honda, N., Pink, M., Wilmot, D., & Wilson, M. (2012). *Constructing measures of teachers' use of formative assessment: An empirical case study of novice teachers in the California middle and high school classroom.* Presented at the California Educational Research Association Conference, Monterey.

Gold, J. (Producer & Director), & Lanzoni, M. (Ed.). (1993). *Graduation by portfolio: Central Park East Secondary School* [Video]. New York: Post Production, 29th Street Video.

Hattie, J. (2012) *Visible learning for teachers: Maximizing impact on learning.* London: Routledge.

Heritage, M. (2008). *Learning progressions: Supporting instruction and formative assessment.* Washington, DC: Council of Chief State School Officers.

Shepard, L. A. (2000). The role of assessment in a learning culture. *Educational Researcher, 29*(7), 4–14.

Stiggins, R. J. (2002). Assessment crisis: The absence of assessment FOR learning. *Phi Delta Kappan, 83*(10), 758–765.

Wiggins, G. (2012). Seven keys to effective feedback. *Educational Leadership, 70*(1), 10–16.

Yin, Y., Tomita, M. K., & Shavelson, R. J. (2008). Diagnosing and dealing with student misconceptions: Floating and sinking. *Science Scope*, 31(8), 34–39.

Zwiers, J. (2007). *Building academic language: Essential practices for content classrooms*. San Francisco: Jossey Bass.

Brent Duckor (brent.duckor@sjsu.edu) is an assistant professor at the Lurie College of Education, San Jose State University, California.

Originally published in the March 2014 issue of *Educational Leadership*, *71*(6): pp. 28–32.

Feed Up, Back, Forward

Douglas Fisher and Nancy Frey

Teacher response is only one part of an effective feedback system. We must also set clear learning goals and let data influence instruction.

Like the sailors in Samuel Coleridge's poem "The Rime of the Ancient Mariner" who see "water, water everywhere, nor any drop to drink," teachers often feel awash in a resource that is of little help. Teachers have more assessment data about individual students at their fingertips than we could have imagined a decade ago. Unlike saltwater to a thirsty mariner, the data are of course highly usable resources for teachers. Yet many feel unable to "drink" the data around them because they don't have a system for processing it.

We recently saw a teacher collect literacy assessment data on her iPhone and then upload the scores instantly into the school's computer. It was impressive. When we asked how she planned to use this information, however, the teacher replied, "It's just a benchmark test I'm required to give; I don't really use the data." Therein lies the problem: A resource that could significantly enhance teaching and learning is left unused.

The solution is twofold. First, educators have to understand the three components of any powerful feedback system. Second, we have to align the multiple measures we use to create a coherent system of data collection, analysis, and instruction that responds to data in a way that lifts student achievement.

What Makes a Strong Feedback System?

Feedback is a powerful way to affect student achievement (Hattie & Timperley, 2007). Research consistently ranks feedback as among the strongest interventions at teachers' disposal (Kluger & DeNisi, 1996). But feedback is a complex construct with at least three distinct components, which we call *feed up*, *feed back*, and *feed forward*. To fully implement a feedback system, teachers must use all three.

Feed Up: Clarify the Goal

The first component of an effective feedback system involves establishing a clear purpose. When students understand the ultimate goal, they are more likely to focus on the learning tasks at hand. Establishing a purpose is also crucial to a feedback system because when teachers have a clear overall purpose, they can align their various assessments. For example, when it's clear that the purpose of a unit is to compare insects and arthropods, students know what to expect and the teacher can plan readings, collaborative projects, investigations, and assessments to ensure that students focus on content related to this goal.

Feed Back: Respond to Student Work

The individual responses teachers give students about their work are the second component of a good feedback system, and the one that is most commonly recognized. These responses should directly relate to the learning goal. The best feedback provides students with information about their progress—or lack of it—toward that goal and suggests actions they can take to come closer to the expected standard (Brookhart, 2008). Ideally, teachers give feedback as students complete discrete tasks that are part of a larger project so that students can use teachers' suggestions to better master content and improve their performance on the larger project.

For example, in a unit on writing high-quality introductions, a teacher gave students multiple opportunities to introduce topics using such techniques as beginning with a question or startling statistic, leading off with an anecdote, and so on. The teacher provided students feedback on each introduction they wrote so students could revise that introduction and use the suggestions to improve their next attempt. Rather than simply noting mechanical errors, the teacher acknowledged areas of success and highlighted things students might focus on sharpening.

Feed Forward: Modify Instruction

This formative aspect of a feedback system is often left out. In an effective feedback system, teachers use assessment data to plan future instruction; hence the term *feed forward*. As teachers look at student work, whether from a checking-for-understanding task or a common formative assessment, they use what they learn to modify their teaching. This demands greater flexibility in lesson planning because it means that teachers can't simply implement a set series of lessons.

For example, student groups in one 3rd grade class we observed each completed a collaborative poster in response to a word problem. Students had to answer the questions in each problem using words, numbers, and pictures. A typical problem read, "Six students are sitting at each table in the lunchroom. There are 23 tables. How many students are in the lunchroom?" Nearly every group got the wrong answer to its problem. Given this information, the teacher knew she needed to provide more modeling to the entire class on how to solve word problems.

Another teacher noted that six of his students regularly capitalized random words in sentences. Mauricio, for example, incorrectly capitalized *fun*, *very*, and *challenge*. Considering that the other students were not making this error, the teacher knew that a whole-class intervention was unnecessary. Instead, he provided additional instruction for the six students who consistently capitalized at random.

Moving Toward Alignment

For a feedback system to be informative, all measures must align with one another to present a rich portrait of how students are progressing toward a common goal. For example, daily checking-for-understanding practices should contribute to a teacher's understanding of how students will perform with similar material in a unit, in a course, and on state assessments. The following practices form a system of assessment experiences that allow for feeding up, feeding back, and feeding forward.

Check for Understanding

At the core of daily teaching is the ability to check for understanding in such a way that teachers learn how to help students. Fostering oral language and using questioning techniques aid this kind of informed check-in (Fisher & Frey, 2007). The evidence on using student talk as a mechanism for learning is compelling; in classrooms with higher rates and levels of student talk, more students excel academically (Stichter, Stormont, & Lewis, 2009).

Language frames help stimulate academic talk in the classroom and also help gauge students' understanding of concepts. Language frames are cloze statements that provide students with the academic language necessary to explain, justify, clarify, and ask for evidence.

In a mathematics lesson, Ms. Kelly introduced her 1st grade English language learners to the language frame "The _____ is _____-er than the _____" to help them contrast the relative size of two objects, a math standard in Ms. Kelly's district. Using a feedup strategy, she explained that the students' purpose was to approximate the size of two objects. She then had the students, in pairs, practice making sentences using this language frame in several different contexts.

On the day we observed Ms. Kelly's class, student pairs were using this frame to compare the sizes of different animals on laminated cards. When Joseph, one of the students, said, "The snake is wider than the duck," his partner Mario asked, "Is the snake wider or narrower than the duck?" to cue Joseph to rethink his answer.

Ms. Kelly let the boys know they needed to approximate more accurately and asked each boy to show the width of each animal with two hands spread apart. Joseph could gesture correctly but could not accurately convert his knowledge to spoken language. Ms. Kelly understood that the barrier was language and not the measurement concept, so she concentrated on reteaching the language frame until Joseph could use it correctly (the feed-forward element).

Questioning is vital to checking for understanding, especially as it pertains to giving feedback on incorrect responses. When faced with a student error, we should remind ourselves that the answer usually makes sense to the student and reflects what he or she knows and does not know at the moment. We can rapidly form a hypothesis about what the student might *not* know to provide a prompt that will help that student achieve the needed understanding. Walsh and Sattes (2005) suggest these follow-up prompts:

- Words or phrases that foster recall ("Think about the role of hydrogen").
- Overt reminders to trigger memory ("The word begins with *d*").
- Probes that elicit the reasoning behind the answer to identify knowledge gaps ("What led you to think the character would do that?")

- A reworded question that reduces language demands. For example, instead of asking a student to "identify the role of tectonic plates in earth geophysical systems," the teacher might say, "Earthquakes and volcanoes have something in common; let's talk about that."

Use Common Assessments

In addition to providing a way to check daily for understanding, an aligned system includes common formative assessments that enable teachers to coordinate with other teachers in their grade level or department. These assessments are usually based on units of instruction and become part of the pacing guide for each course. Such benchmark assessments gauge increments of student performance and provide teachers with data that spur conversation about instructional and curricular design.

We recommend that teachers meet in advance of teaching a unit to develop common formative assessments. The assessment items teachers select should be geared to diagnose specific kinds of learning so that teachers can discuss any misconceptions students still hold after instruction and recognize patterns among students (Fisher, Grant, Frey, & Johnson, 2007). Teachers should meet as soon as possible after they score each assessment to discuss the relationship between the results and teachers' instruction and to plan next steps (the feed-forward component).

Partial conceptual understanding is a common cause of incorrect responses. For example, Ms. Goldstein's English as a second language class was studying affixes in preparation for a benchmark assessment. Ms. Goldstein explained that the lesson's purpose was to analyze new vocabulary words (feed up). Omar incorrectly identified *in-* as the prefix for *interlude*. Rather than simply supply Omar with the correct answer and move on, Ms. Goldstein asked him what the prefixes *in-* and *inter-* meant and received a correct reply. "Could the root be '*-lude*,' or is it '*-terlude*'?" Ms. Goldstein questioned. Omar stayed with his initial incorrect answer, so she tried again, asking Omar's small group, "Is the prefix *in-* or *inter-*? I'll let you figure it out" (providing feedback that something needed to be figured out).

Omar's group talked about the two meanings and how they would affect the overall word. Ms. Goldstein checked a few minutes later on whether Omar and his group had arrived at the correct answer.

After the English as a second language department administered its common formative assessment on affixes, Ms. Goldstein remarked, "I noticed some students in my class getting similar prefixes like *in-* and *inter-* confused. This was a pattern in all our classes. How can we teach look-alike prefixes more effectively?" The teachers decided to develop a Jeopardy-style game that included easily confounded affixes to give students practice.

Identify Competencies

Although unit-based formative assessments are valuable benchmarks to inform teachers' instruction, they offer students only snapshots of their progress. Learners need a system to measure their own attainment of course goals. Goals should be a balance of short-term ("I'm going to ask good questions today") and long-term ("I'll pass biology"); however, the gap between short-term and long-term goals can be overwhelming. Creating a system of specific competencies that students should achieve in a course and a series of assessments that measure those competencies and provide clear feedback enable students to measure their progress through any course.

Grade-level teams or departments usually specify course competencies and corresponding assignments. Competencies should reflect the state standards while offering students an array of ways to demonstrate mastery, not just paper-and-pencil tasks. The competency assessments should be numerous enough that students can adequately gauge their own progress at attaining competencies; generally 7 to 10 per academic year is best.

Ninth and 10th grade English teachers at one high school devised a series of 10 competency assessments for their common courses. These included four essays based on schoolwide essential questions, two literary response essays, an oral language assessment that included retelling a story and delivering a dramatic monologue, a poetry portfolio, and tests on persuasive writing techniques and summarizing.

These teachers designed a two-week unit on plagiarizing that, as they explained to students in a "feed-up" message, would help them write their formal essays. The teachers developed a common formative assessment that measured how well students could cite information from a newspaper article, a Web site, a book with two or more authors, and an interview. The results indicated that even after studying plagiarism, many students still couldn't correctly cite online sources. Knowing that students would need this competency to write their first essay, teachers analyzed students' incorrect answers and retaught the specifics of this type of online citation accordingly.

Build Toward State Assessments

An aligned system of assessments should build toward helping students do well on state tests that measure the progress of students and schools. Although we do not believe a few weeks crammed with test-prep worksheets are useful, we do believe that students should understand that tests are a genre, one they are capable of mastering. And we advocate assessment practices that build test wiseness by giving students encounters with test formats in the context of meaningful instruction.

For example, a math teacher might model thinking aloud as she eliminates distractors on multiple-choice questions. When faced with the problem 1/7 + 3/7 and three answer choices of 4/7, 3/7, and 4/14, the teacher might say, "I see one of the choices has 14 as a denominator.

But I know you don't add the denominator when adding fractions so that can't be correct." When teachers embed test-format practice within daily checking for understanding, formative assessments, and course competency exams, students acquire the stamina and skills they need to score well on state assessments.

What the Mariner Teaches Us

"The Rime of the Ancient Mariner" is a cautionary tale about failing to learn from one's mistakes. The mariner was doomed to walk the earth telling strangers that he had killed an albatross that had saved his ship from disaster. If educators view data as a liability simply because we don't know what to do with that data, we risk ignoring something that may help us. By viewing assessment as a system that gives us the power to feed up, feed back, and feed forward, we can avoid mistaking help for hindrance.

Editor's note: All names are pseudonyms.

References

Brookhart, S. M. (2008). *How to give effective feedback to your students.* Alexandria, VA: ASCD.

Fisher, D., & Frey, N. (2007). *Checking for understanding: Formative assessment techniques for your classroom.* Alexandria, VA: ASCD.

Fisher, D., Grant, M., Frey, N., & Johnson, C. (2007). Taking formative assessments schoolwide. *Educational Leadership, 65*(4), 64–68.

Hattie, J., & Timperley, H. (2007). The power of feedback. *Review of Educational Research, 77,* 81–112.

Kluger, A. N., & DeNisi, A. (1996). The effects of feedback interventions on performance: A historical review, a meta-analysis, and a preliminary feedback intervention theory. *Psychological Bulletin, 119*(2), 254–284.

Stichter, J. P., Stormont, M., & Lewis, T. J. (2009). Instructional practices and behavior during reading: A descriptive summary and comparison of practices in Title 1 and non-title elementary schools. *Psychology in the Schools, 46*(2), 172–183.

Walsh, J. A., & Sattes, B. D. (2005). *Quality questioning: Research-based practices to engage every learner.* Thousand Oaks, CA: Corwin.

Douglas Fisher (dfisher@mail.sdsu.edu) is Professor of Literacy and **Nancy Frey** (nfrey@mail.sdsu.edu) is Associate Professor of Literacy at San Diego State University in California.

Originally published in the November 2009 issue of *Educational Leadership, 67*(3): pp. 20–25.

The Right Questions, The Right Way

Dylan Wiliam

What do the questions teachers ask in class
really reveal about student learning?

It is perhaps the most familiar of all classroom routines: A teacher asks the class a question, several students raise their hands, the teacher selects one of those with a hand raised, the student gives a response, the teacher evaluates the student's response, and the cycle begins again. Education researchers call it the *standard classroom transaction model* or just *I-R-E* (for initiation-response-evaluation). You will find this model played out it in the vast majority of classrooms in every country in the world. Teachers use this routine to assess where students are so that they can plan next steps. Yet just about every aspect of this scenario actually gets in the way of learning—and it doesn't provide enough information on what most students in the class know and need to learn.

What's Wrong with the Traditional Routine?

The fundamental flaw in the traditional questioning model is that it makes participation voluntary. The confident students engage by raising their hands—and by engaging in classroom discussion, they become smarter. But others decline the invitation to participate and thus miss out on the chance to get smarter.

This creates what Keith Stanovich (1986) once called an educational *Matthew effect*, an idea drawn from the biblical passage that reads, "For the one who has will be given more, and he will have more than enough. But the one who does not have, even what he has will be taken from him" (Matthew 25:29). Psychologists call it the multiplier effect, made famous by Malcolm Gladwell (2008) in his book *Outliers*. The oldest children in their grade experience early success, which leads to greater effort, which leads to still greater success. The younger students feel unsuccessful and often concentrate on other pursuits.

A second problem with the traditional approach is that even if a teacher chooses students at random, the teacher will only be assessing the understanding of one or two students. Making an instructional decision about what to do next with a class on the basis of the responses of one or two students is unlikely to be a recipe for success.

The third problem with the standard questioning model is that teachers rarely plan the questions they use. When, as teachers, we ask questions and get the answers we were hoping for, we generally conclude that students' learning is on track. But if the questions have not been carefully planned, there is a real danger of concluding that the students are on the right track when, in fact, their understanding of the subject is quite different from what we intend.

There are solutions to these problems that any teacher can implement, at little or no cost. These solutions have been known for years, yet they are still rare in classrooms.

No Hands Up

Perhaps the simplest way to improve classroom questioning is simply not to ask for volunteers, but instead to choose a student at random.

Students raise their hands only to ask questions, not to answer them. Such a move is unpopular—teachers find it difficult to manage, students who used to raise their hands in response to every question can't show off their knowledge, and students who used to have a quiet life now have to pay attention. But in terms of small changes that can have big effects, "no hands up" may be the most significant thing a teacher can do.

Selecting students at random is more difficult than teachers think. When time is tight, teachers are often drawn to "the usual suspects" for a good strong response. This is why some sort of randomization device is helpful. Many interactive whiteboards have randomizers built into the software, randomizers can be downloaded from the Internet, and there are even smartphone apps for randomizing. However, for random questioning, it is hard to beat students' names on tongue depressors.

Many teachers prefer to choose the student first and then ask the question, but this is generally a bad idea, because as soon as students know who is going to have to respond to the question, all the other students can relax. It is far better to ask the question first, give students time to think of a response, and then pick a student at random to respond.

The danger here is that the teacher will select a student for whom the question is too easy or too hard. There is certainly no point in asking a student a question the teacher knows the student cannot answer, but when teachers assume they know which students can answer and which cannot, they tend to produce self-fulfilling prophecies. As one student I interviewed about "no hands up" said, "I never knew my classmates were so smart."

One way to make questions suitable for any student is to pose them in a way that allows students to engage with the question at a number of different levels. For example, rather than asking students to answer a math question, the teacher could pose two questions of differing difficulty on the board and ask, "Which of these two questions is harder and why?" The ensuing discussion will raise all the important mathematical issues that the teacher needs to cover, but the question has been posed in an inclusive way that enables more students to contribute, thus supporting differentiated instruction.

As the work of James T. Dillon (1988) has shown, it is particularly effective to forgo questions entirely and instead make statements to which students are expected to respond. Through follow-up, the teacher can deal with any misunderstanding or other issue that the response reveals without "wrong-footing" students from the outset.

For example, rather than asking students in a world history class, "Which country was most to blame for the outbreak of World War I?" which is likely to have students just plumping for different countries, the teacher might make the statement, "Russia was most to blame for the outbreak of World War I," and expect students to react. And rather than saying, "What do you mean by that?" the teacher could say, "I'm confused by what you're saying." The differences are small, but research by Dillon and others shows that these small changes can have a big effect on the length and depth of student responses.

The whole idea that students should always answer teachers' questions correctly is actually rather odd. If the students are answering every one of the teacher's questions correctly, the teacher is surely wasting the students' time. If the questions are not causing students to struggle and think, they are probably not worth asking. As I say to students, "Mistakes are evidence that the questions I asked are tough enough to make you smarter." Of course, the best teachers have always said that making mistakes is OK, but recent research has shown that making mistakes in learning is actually better than not making mistakes (Huelser & Metcalfe, 2012). When students are taught material and tested on their recall, the students who did badly on the test and are shown their mistakes and the correct answers are the students who score best on a post-test weeks later.

The no-hands-up approach can make discussions more engaging, but this approach still only assesses the learning of a few students.

To plan next steps, teachers need information from every student in the class.

All-Student Response Systems

In higher education, electronic voting systems or "clickers" have enabled professors to make their lectures much more interactive. However, in classrooms of 20 to 30 students, the cost of the necessary equipment and the time required to set it up may outweigh the benefits. In addition, the fact that electronic voting systems enable the teacher to have a record of every response made by every student seems to be at variance with the idea of the classroom as a safe place for making mistakes.

I prefer low-tech solutions for quickly assessing student understanding: ABCD cards students hold up to answer multiple-choice questions, dry-erase boards students write answers on, and having students hold up a number of fingers. None of these ideas is new. After all, the dry-erase board is simply the 21st century's version of the student slate. The powerful thing about all these approaches is that the teacher can quickly scan the students' responses and make an immediate decision about what to do next.

To make scanning easier, I recommend the use of multiple-choice questions. If a teacher asks students to write their own answers to a question on dry-erase boards, the teacher has a complex data-processing task: making sense of 30 idiosyncratic responses in seconds. However, if the teacher asks a multiple-choice question, the potential variety of the students' responses is more manageable.

The problem with multiple-choice questions is that they take time to construct, and it is practically impossible to invent a good multiple-choice question on the fly. Yet if students write more than three words each on a dry-erase board, then in a class of 30, the teacher has over 100 words to read, so it's important to keep it simple. If a question is likely to require a longer response, then it may be more appropriate to issue each student an index card and ask students to write their responses on the card. If this is done toward the end of a lesson, the teacher can ask students to hand in these "exit passes" as they leave the class.

If the students turn in the cards anonymously, then the teacher can just make a decision about where to begin the next lesson. If, however, the students write their names on their cards, the teacher can assign students to sit at different tables for the beginning of the next lesson, either by grouping students with significant misunderstandings at one table and working with them while the rest of the class works on extension material or by creating mixed-ability groups so students can compare responses and help one another.

Planning Questions

When teachers plan lessons, they generally plan, in considerable detail, the kinds of activities in which they will engage the students, the learning intentions of the lesson, and a number of other features. It's far less common for teachers to plan the questions they will use to determine whether the instruction has succeeded. The result is that questions often do not reveal important aspects of students' thinking, and therefore important misunderstandings go undetected. When teachers are aware of common student misunderstandings, they can construct questions ahead of time that reveal where students are confused.

For example, consider the following mathematics question.

Simplify the following fraction: $\frac{16}{64}$

If a student (correctly) responds that the fraction can be simplified to $\frac{1}{4}$, many teachers would conclude that the student understands how to simplify fractions. However, some students simplify this fraction not by realizing that the denominator is four times as large as the numerator, but by "cancelling" the sixes in the numerator and denominator: $\frac{16}{64}$. In this case, an incorrect strategy leads to a correct response. With a different question, such as being asked to simplify $^{24}/_{48}$, the student using this method would respond with $^{2}/_{8}$, and we would realize there is something wrong.

In English language arts, students may answer questions correctly by using a rule that any word that ends in -*ly* is an adverb, which works much of the time but not with words like *leisurely* or *lovely*. Using one of those words in a question about parts of speech will reveal students' incomplete understanding.

In science, young children can often appear to distinguish living things from nonliving things on the basis of whether they move. Such a naïve strategy will yield the correct answer if students are asked whether rocks, cats, or birds are living, but not if the teacher asks whether buses, computers, trees, or grass are living. We want students with the right thinking and students with the wrong thinking to give us different answers. If students with the right thinking and students with the wrong thinking give us the same answer, the question is not particularly useful.

Planning questions is especially important when teaching academic subjects because we cannot peer into students' brains to see what is going on. When a right-handed student throws a baseball standing with the right foot in front of the left, or when a violin student holds the bow with the hand below the bow rather than above, it's obvious what is going wrong. But with academic subjects, we have to elicit evidence of student thinking so that we can give useful feedback. When people think about formative assessment, they usually think about feedback, but you can't give good feedback until you find out what's going wrong in the first place.

A Good Place to Start

Questioning and discussion are key aspects of teachers' work in classrooms, and yet too often, classroom discussions involve only the most confident students, ignore what is happening in the heads of those not volunteering to participate, and rely on prompts and questions that have not been planned in advance. By picking students at random and by using all-student response systems at least once in every 20 to 30 minutes of group instruction, teachers can ensure that their decisions are based on the learning needs of the whole class. By planning their questions, teachers can ensure they are tapping into deep issues of learning, rather than skating across the surface.

These three ideas—no hands up, all-student response systems, and planning questions—are not the only, or even the most, important aspects of teaching. Trying to manage the learning that is happening in 30 different minds at the same time will always be extraordinarily challenging. But by increasing the engagement of students, and thus improving the feedback from the teacher, we can make a real difference. One teacher described the process as making the students' voices louder and making the teacher's hearing better. Sounds like a good place to start.

References

Dillon, J. T. (1988). *Questioning and teaching: A manual of practice*. London: Croom Helm.

Gladwell, M. (2008). *Outliers: The story of success*. New York: Little, Brown.

Huelser, B. J., & Metcalfe, J. (2012). Making related errors facilitates learning, but learners do not know it. *Memory and Cognition, 40*(4), 514–527.

Stanovich, K. E. (1986). Matthew effects in reading: Some consequences of individual differences in the acquisition of literacy. *Reading Research Quarterly, 21*(4), 360–407.

Dylan Wiliam (dylanwiliam@mac.com) lives in New Jersey and is Emeritus Professor of Educational Assessment at the Institute of Education, University of London. He is the author of *Embedded Formative Assessment* (Solution Tree, 2011).

Originally published in the March 2014 issue of *Educational Leadership, 71*(6): pp. 16–19.

The New Teacher's Guide to Better Assessment

Mary Jo Grdina

School leaders can improve their teachers' assessment
practices by providing sound guidance along the way.

Let's start with a simple assessment of your ability to evaluate some pieces of art. Below, you'll find photographs of three pieces of Steuben glass. Steuben has been designing luxury handcrafted crystal since 1903. Your task is to rank the three pieces in order of increasing market value.

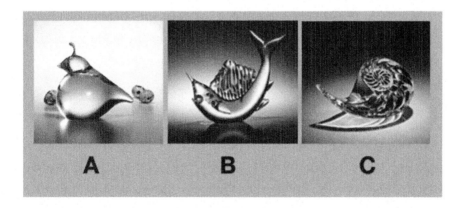

Write down your value rankings before you check the answers at the end of this article.

How well did you do? Was the task difficult? If so, perhaps it's because you had limited information about each piece. You were not given any dimensions—one piece could be much larger than the other two—and you were only given one view of the three-dimensional pieces. Your design taste could also have influenced your ranking. Some people like sleek lines (choice a, *Quintessential Quail*); others are attracted to drama (choice b, *Sailfish*) or to nature's symmetries (choice c, *Nautilus Shell*). Even if you had been given more information on each piece and had no preference for the objects depicted, you may have fallen short in this task because you have no experience evaluating artistic glass.

The points I make in this simple exercise are analogous to important considerations in evaluating students. We have often heard that tests are only snapshots. I could hardly evaluate your skills at analyzing art on the basis of that exercise alone. In the same way, we need so much more information than tests can provide before we can judge whether a student is an analytical reader, a creative writer, or an advanced placement–level mathematician. In addition, despite those well-constructed rubrics we use, are we truly objective in our student evaluations—or are we sometimes, as in this glass-ranking exercise, influenced by personal taste?

School leaders can ensure that teachers avoid common pitfalls and hone their skills in using sound assessments by leading a school-wide effort that focuses on improving assessment practices.

The Real Aim of Assessment

As a curriculum supervisor and college professor in a school of education, my job is to train future teachers. State certification and other standards require that in their portfolios, graduates demonstrate their ability to generate formative and summative assessments that address a variety of learning styles and accommodate the needs of special learners. Graduates often leave their teacher education programs with idealistic visions of the range of assessments they will use to evaluate their students.

But what may *really* happen to these new teachers when they enter the workforce? Some may have a teacher like Harriet as a mentor. A well-respected veteran, Harriet teaches science to more than 100 high school students. When progress reports are due and she needs more grades, she decides to give her biology students a test, an old one from last year. She realizes that she hasn't covered all the material on this test yet, but she's pressed for time. It's also multiple choice, so it will be easy to correct. The fact is, even seasoned teachers like Harriet, who put serious time and effort into their lesson designs, often resort to more efficient, rather than more effective, assessment instruments.

So how can we preserve the ideals of new teachers when they enter the hectic real world of teaching? And how can we convince veteran teachers that the aim of assessment is to educate and improve, not merely to audit student performance (Wiggins, 1998)?

School leaders can do this by taking three important steps.

Step 1: Start with Coaching

Too often, administrators use a one-size-fits-all approach to professional development, which can lead to teacher annoyance and frustration. If we are going to encourage our teachers to be mindful of addressing the needs of diverse learners, then we should be mindful of the needs of diverse teachers.

Once we have clarified where we want our teachers to be as effective evaluators of student performance, we must then determine where they are along the continuum. Do teachers willingly look for opportunities to improve? Are they open to constructive criticism? Do they realize what an awesome task student evaluation is? Identifying teachers' strengths and weaknesses is essential in designing successful mentoring and coaching strategies.

Many factors contribute to a teacher's competence in assessment. The number of years that the teacher has spent in the classroom does not necessarily correlate directly with an ability to evaluate students. An experienced teacher who does not see a reason to change the way he or she has always graded students will need different guidance than the new teacher who has been trained in designing rubrics but lacks the organizational skills to do so efficiently.

This individualized approach requires time. Administrators need to recognize and believe in coaching as a way to help teachers succeed. It's also an integral part of creating a community of intellectual and self-motivated educators.

Step 2: Question Your Teachers

Once teachers have made a commitment to improve the assessment process, they need some support. Accountability is key to helping teachers grow—and asking questions is a crucial part of that process. For example, as teachers, we let our students know what we think is important by asking such questions as, Did you check your work for spelling errors? Have you looked at this problem from more than one angle?

As school leaders, we also let our teachers know what we think is important by the questions we ask them. Ask your teachers to do the following:

Include sample assessments with their lesson plans.

Every school has a protocol for submitting weekly lesson plans. When I was a high school math teacher, for many years I submitted a plan book the week before I taught the lessons. I conscientiously filled in the boxes with lesson objectives, references to state standards, an outline of lesson activities, and a list of assignments. Often the words *quiz* or *unit test* would fill a box. Only once in my long career was I asked to submit a sample of a quiz or test; I was never asked to submit a grading rubric.

Some teachers might react negatively to this request because they will understandably perceive it as yet another pointless thing to do. However, if you do not ask, how will they know it's important? If you collect and code these assessments for one month, you will get a better handle on how teachers evaluate the students in your school. In addition, teachers will more carefully examine their assessment practices.

Highlight verbs in lesson objectives.

Early in my teaching career, I was given a list of verbs from Bloom's taxonomy to assist me in working on a curriculum committee. This was the first time I became aware of a taxonomy of higher-order thinking skills. This document, now worn around the edges, is still an important reference on my desk.

Highlighting the verbs used in the lesson objectives will help both new and seasoned teachers focus on goals that are higher than mere knowledge acquisition. Ask your teachers the following questions: Which levels of higher-level thinking are you addressing in your lessons? What do you really mean by *understand* (Wiggins, 1998)? Do your assessments really provide "acceptable evidence" (Wiggins & McTighe, 2005)?

This last question is crucial to improving student evaluation. If a unit goal states that "the student will be able to show the relationships among the functions of different organelles in an animal cell," having students label the parts of a cell is not acceptable evidence that the students have mastered that goal. Carefully crafting good assessments and the accompanying rubrics takes time and talent. Teachers may need time and training to do this well. Training can begin at a faculty, department, or grade-level meeting. Teachers could share lesson plans and assessments that show correlation between the verbs in unit objectives and the questions asked on the unit test or the rubrics used for grading the unit project.

Another simple and valuable exercise is to ask teachers to high-light the verbs in national and state standards. Many have looked at the content identified in standards; not all have looked at the level of critical thought involved.

Share best practices and help one another.

If formalized peer mentoring and action research programs seem beyond what you can currently ask of your teachers, you can still use regularly scheduled faculty meeting time to let teachers talk. Too often details, such as homecoming issues or fire drill procedures, consume meeting times. There is an unspoken message here about what we value most.

I have also witnessed poor teacher behavior during presentations made by outside experts, either during faculty meetings or special in-service programs. As administrators, we should ask, How can we keep teachers actively engaged in meetings? We preach against the "sage on the stage" model in the classroom and encourage "the guide on the side" approach. Could we also apply this approach to the way we run faculty, department, or grade-level meetings?

Teachers can learn from one another. Experts in the group can lead collaborative growth by sharing their assessment strategies. We do not always need to bring someone in from outside. A simple think-pair-share activity at a faculty meeting can yield amazing results.

Step 3: Focus on Assessment Balance

Some new research-based programs offer helpful assessment tools. For example, *Everyday Mathematics* includes a tool called a quad that a teacher in any content area can use to develop an individualized assessment plan and chart assessment balance (Everyday Mathematics Assessment Handbooks, 2004). This circle graph, which shows the proportion of different assessment types, consists of four segments: outside tests, periodic assessments, product assessments, and ongoing assessments. Outside tests include district and state assessments and standardized achievement tests, periodic assessments include teacher-constructed quizzes and unit tests, performance assessments refer to portfolio-type items, and ongoing assessments include observations of students as they work on regular classroom activities.

The size of each segment will vary with grade level and teacher. For example, ongoing assessment will be a large piece during a student's early years when teacher observation is most useful for monitoring student progress. Having teachers calculate and construct a quad to include in their teaching portfolios or annual assessment observations achieves two desirable goals: While preparing the diagrams, the teachers must quantitatively examine the importance they give to each type of assessment, and the final visual product gives the evaluator a clear graphic that shows patterns and changes in the way a teacher evaluates students.

A Matter of Will

Art critic and social thinker John Ruskin once said, "Quality is never an accident. It is always the result of intelligent effort. There must be the will to produce a superior thing."

School leaders are responsible for producing this "superior thing"—and for making teachers aware what an awesome responsibility student evaluation is. They can do this by breaking assessment down into a series of measurable benchmarks. And they can start with these three steps.

Author's note: Current market prices for the pieces are: (a) Quintessential Quail: $1,500; (b) Sailfish: $3,100; (c)Nautilus Shell: $300. Illustrations courtesy of Steuben Glass.

References

Everyday Mathematics Assessment Handbooks. (2004). Chicago: SRA/ McGraw-Hill.

Wiggins, G. (1998). *Educative assessment: Designing assessments to inform and improve student performance.* San Francisco: Jossey-Bass.

Wiggins, G., & McTighe, J. (2005). *Understanding by design (expanded 2nd ed.).* Alexandria, VA: ASCD.

Mary Jo Grdina (maryjo.f.grdina@drexel.edu) is Associate Clinical Professor of Education in the School of Education at Drexel University.

Originally published online in the November 2009 issue of *Educational Leadership, 67*(3).

12

How I Broke My Rule and Learned to Give Retests

Myron Dueck

*Structured choices for retesting can
motive even the lowest achievers.*

Six years ago, a conference on standards-based grading and assessment left me with the distinct and slightly confounding sense that my
assessment procedures needed to change. As it turned out, one of the
assessment practices I had been most wedded to was one I eventually
overturned.

   The conference, which my principal at the high school where I
then taught urged me to attend, reinforced nagging questions I'd long
had about traditional grading practices. During the first sessions, I
agreed in whole or part with nearly everything presenters said. For
years, I'd encouraged students to make practice tests, so the concept of
formative assessment was familiar to me. Like the presenters, I'd faced
the conundrum of how to equitably grade the bright student who did
little homework but scored high on tests, and I'd felt uneasy with the
practice of reducing grades for assignments that were handed in late.

Then a speaker prompted me to question one of my most entrenched rules: *Never* offer retests.

On my flight home, as I reflected on what I'd learned, I realized how much retests would collide with the grading procedures I used as a high school history teacher. I saw two obvious stumbling blocks to offering retests: (1) My courses were very content-heavy, and I had little time to spend on retests; and (2) I didn't know how to maintain an authentic measure of learning if I allowed everyone to take retests.

Pondering how to make it work, I thought of the model of assessment Rick Stiggins had presented. His model made sense to me, especially the three key questions he said students must know how to answer. At the beginning of a unit, all students should be able to answer the question, Where are we going? After an assessment, they should be able to answer the question, Where am I? and after answering both of these questions, the student should be able to answer, How do I close the gap?[1] I used these questions as touchstones as I transformed my testing policy.

Smooth Sailing on "Where Are We Going"?

With a little help from my vice principal at the time, Tom Schimmer, this was a relatively easy question to address. In his previous school, Tom had been using student-friendly unit plans that clearly delineated *learning targets*—what a student needed to be able to do during each unit. I began using learning targets in my senior history courses. I laid out all unit requirements under one of the following headings:

- Knowledge Targets: What do I need to know?
- Reasoning Targets: What can I do with what I know?
- Skill Targets: What can I demonstrate?
- Product Targets: What can I make to show my learning?

I presented each target as an "I can" statement, which made it easier for students to understand the target and take ownership of reaching it.

Both my students and I found these unit plans incredibly helpful. In the knowledge targets section, students could find all the "Trivial Pursuit" objectives—definitions, dates, names, and other specific information they needed to know. I explained to students that these knowledge pieces were essential to success in the course; any discussion or activity we did in the unit would require them to know these core facts. For example, one knowledge target for our pre–World War II unit was "I can list four conditions in 1930s Germany that resulted in Hitler gaining power."

Reasoning targets reflect what students can do with what they know. In my courses, these are often the most interesting targets, as students are required to bring knowledge pieces together to form an argument or make a judgment. Terms such as *justify, determine, compare,* and *evaluate* are commonly found in this section. An example of a reasoning target from the pre–World War II unit might be "I can explain to what extent the United States followed a policy of isolationism in the 1930s."

Skill and product targets are relatively easy to determine. Skill targets focus on what students can do to demonstrate understanding, such as make a speech or complete a hands-on map activity. One student's skill target for the pre–World War II history unit was "I can research a member of the Jewish community living in 1930s Germany and give a two-minute speech on his or her specific concerns or challenges." Product targets refer to what students make to show learning; for example, a short written description, PowerPoint presentation, or collage of images that represent the social conditions of the 1930s.

My students reacted very positively to these structures. At the end of each unit, we went over the unit's plan as a class. (In one case, we discovered that we'd missed covering a knowledge target because a fire drill took us out of class!) Students used the targets as study guides by checking off the "I can" statements and determining what they still needed to learn. As one student noted, "I'm able to discover what I know and don't know before I take the test."

Hitting Bumps at "Where Am I?"

I thought students could answer this question as they always had—by seeing their graded tests and my feedback. The new element would be that students could close the gap by further study followed by a retest. I believed I could administer retests using my existing test structure and rely on my comments to guide students toward improvement. It turned out to be more complicated.

With some trepidation, on returning a set of tests, I announced to my History 12 students that students who were unhappy with their results could see me after class to schedule a retest. Allie was one student who requested a retest, and we arranged a lunch meeting for the following day.

Before her appointment, I looked over Allie's test, and I knew I had a problem. The test consisted of a few sections. Allie requested to focus only on the first section of 40 multiple-choice questions, in which she had 12 errors. Given the complexity of the question format and the integration of different learning objectives into different sections, I couldn't ascertain specifically where her weaknesses lay. Consequently, I couldn't determine an efficient and accurate way to retest Allie. Even if I asked a complete second set of random questions and Allie rewrote the whole test, I still couldn't guarantee that her second assessment would be a clear replacement of the first.

I ended up interviewing Allie on the individual questions she had missed, trying to see whether she now understood them better. It was a painful, inefficient process that lasted 30 minutes and didn't give either of us much insight. I was left with the clear understanding that I'd better revamp this process.

As a first step, I reorganized my tests. Rather than sticking with my usual formula of separating each test into sections by type of question—multiple choice, short answer, long answer—I rethought my structure. I settled on separating sections by learning outcomes/major topics and varying the type of questions within each of these sections. For example, my test on Franklin Delano Roosevelt (FDR) resulted in the following sections and values:

- The United States in the 1920s: 11 points
- Causes of the Depression: 4 points
- FDR's efforts to end the Depression: 5 points
- Reactions to FDR's New Deal: 7 points
- The End of the Depression: 6 points

Section 1, for instance, included eight multiple-choice questions and a paragraph worth 3 points that students wrote to a prompt, for a total of 11 points. Section 3 consisted only of definitions. As I constructed each section, it dawned on me to simultaneously write the corresponding section to the "sister" test. While I had my head wrapped around causes of the Depression, for instance, it was easy to make another section on the same topic, also worth 4 points. By the time I was finished, I had two tests with the same sections and values, but different questions.

After my students took the first FDR test, I graded it as usual. When I handed it back, however, the routine changed. I gave each student a tracking sheet (see Figure 12.1) on which I had listed the different sections and values of the test. I had students write in the points they scored on each section and tabulate their percentage score. The last box beside each section was where students indicated whether they intended to retake that section. Within a few minutes, students

Figure 12.1: Tracking Sheet

Franklin Delano Roosevelt   **History 12**

Name: Jon Black   Date: April 3, 2010

Topic	Value	Score	%	Retest?
The USA in the 1920s	11	8	73%	
Causes of the Depression	4	3	75%	
FDR's efforts to end the Depression	5	2	40%	✓
Reactions to FDR's New Deal	7	7	100%	
The End of the Depression	6	3	50%	✓

Total points 23 out of 33. Overall score: 70%

Unit Terms/Preparation

☐ I DID complete all of the terms for this unit on either cards or sheets.
☑ I DID NOT complete either the cards or the term list for this unit.
    Reason: I didn't think I needed to; I felt prepared
☐ I DID complete a different form of preparation. Explain: _____

Goals and Strategies

What **overall grade** (percentage or letter) am I hoping to achieve
in this course? 85%

☐ I did all that I could to achieve my goal in preparing for this test.
☑ I plan to make the following adjustments to increase my grade:

    ✓ Complete all vocabulary cards
    ✓ Make practice quiz to test myself

had a graphic representation of their strengths and weaknesses on each learning outcome. Because students actively tabulated their own section scores, the classroom atmosphere was a far cry from the disengaged atmosphere so common when teachers return tests.

Progressing Toward Closing the Gap

While I had my students' attention, I included on each tracking sheet questions about their test preparation, study skills, and goal setting, and then collected the completed sheets. I found that some students admittedly struggled to study effectively. Looking over the sheets, I could determine which students were—and weren't—using my suggested study routines. If students were not doing assigned homework or not taking time to study, when appropriate I made these actions prerequisites for a retest.

I returned a copy of their tracking sheet to all students who requested a retest. Each student went home with a copy of his or her section scores, a list of which sections to study for the retest, and a summary of suggested study routines.

We scheduled students' retests during class or at lunchtime. Some students selected to retest only one section, others chose to retackle multiple sections, and some left their test score as it was. I offered topic-specific tutorials on areas students missed, at lunch or after school.

At first, struggling learners often chose to retest only one section. I took this opportunity to converse with each struggler about preparation and study techniques and to urge him or her to put in an extra study session independently or schedule a session with me. Because extra studying focused on only one section or topic, the at-risk learner usually perceived it as easier and shorter and was willing. As low-scoring students began to see dramatic improvement on their retested sections, many displayed heightened levels of confidence and tackled multiple sections on subsequent retests.

This procedure was also a good tool to assess my teaching. If I noticed that most students scored low on a particular section, I took that as a sign that my instruction on that section might need adjustment. As a class, we have revisited and relearned particular sections and I've scheduled whole-class retests.

A Few Observations

Since I started revamping my testing procedures, I've seen more examples of how the change benefits students and gathered more insights than I could share in one short article. But here are a few of my observations:

- The ability to retest on specific learning outcomes benefits both low- and high-achieving students. When a struggling learner sees a score of 80–100 percent on one section after a retake, I've observed considerable improvements in his or her overall disposition and confidence. On the other hand, high-achieving students living under pressure to keep performing well report less temptation to cheat when they know they'll have a second chance.

- By examining test items and students' performance on retakes, I can often determine whether a student's low test scores are a knowledge issue or related to the question format. For instance, if a student scores low on multiple-choice responses in all sections but high on other question types, that learner likely needs help in strategizing how to answer multiple-choice items.

- You may need to convince peers—and students—of the wisdom of retests. Academically elite students sometimes object to a retesting system because they have become protective of systems that only value those who score well on an initial test. In terms of convincing colleagues, I've found that educators who object to retests have considerable difficulty coming up with any examples of assessments in the "real world" that don't have a retesting component.

Since I reshaped my testing procedures, I've looked into the assessment literature and realized that many researchers conclude that the kind of changes I've made increase students' involvement, achievement, and motivation.[2] I'm glad I've seen it with my own eyes.

Endnotes

[1] Stiggins, R. J., Arter, J., Chappuis, S., & Chappuis, J. (2004). *Classroom assessment for student learning: Doing it right, using it well.* Portland, OR: Assessment Training Institute.

[2] O'Connor, K. (2011). *A repair kit for grading—15 fixes for broken grades* (2nd ed.). Boston: Pearson.

Myron Dueck (myrondueck@gmail.com) is a vice principal and teacher in School District 67 in Penticton, British Columbia. He presents frequently on grading and assessment procedures. He is also author of the book *Grading Smarter, Not Harder: Assessment Strategies That Motivate Kids and Help Them Learn* (ASCD, 2014).

Originally published in the November 2011 issue of *Educational Leadership, 69*(3): pp. 72–75.

Study Guide for
On Formative Assessment:
Readings from Educational Leadership

Naomi Thiers and Teresa Preston

Ideas to try out individually or in a study group.

If teachers are to guide students to learn, they need to know where students are and what they need to do to improve. Likewise, if students are going to learn, they need teacher feedback on their work. *EL* authors offer lots of ideas for assessing students and giving feedback so they can move forward in their learning.

Using Data

Thomas R. Guskey ("How Classroom Assessments Improve Learning") suggests that teachers use the results of assessments to reteach what students got wrong. "This second chance helps determine the effectiveness of the corrective instruction and offers students another opportunity to experience success in learning," he writes. Do you and your colleagues use assessments for this purpose? What are the short- and long-term drawbacks and benefits of using classroom assessments?

The Purpose of Assessment

The title of Carol Ann Tomlinson's article, "The Bridge Between Today's Lesson and Tomorrow's," expresses what formative assessment should be. Such assessment must be aligned with each day's lessons; therefore, it's unlikely to be available as part of a packaged set of assessments given monthly or quarterly. Formative assessment is a day-by-day endeavor.

- Describe your experiences with formative assessment. How well have these assessments fit Tomlinson's definition?
- Read through Tomlinson's 10 principles for formative assessment. Think of a time when you've seen one of the principles applied particularly effectively—either in your classroom or the classroom of a colleague. What effect did following this principle have on teaching and learning?
- Choose one of the principles that you'd like to focus on in the coming weeks. Make a plan for applying it to your own teaching—or for encouraging its application among teachers you lead.
- Tomlinson says that effective teachers are habitual students of their students. How are you a student of your students? How do you routinely gather information about your students, and how do you use that information to plan instruction?

The Keys to Feedback

In his article, "Seven Keys to Effective Feedback," Grant Wiggins writes that feedback is not a value judgment, nor is it advice. Rather, feedback is information about the progress a person is making toward a goal. It might include direct observations of the direct results of one's actions, as when a tennis player observes whether she has kept the ball on the court. Or it may include observations from an outsider, as when a reader tells a writer how an essay made him feel.

Read the following statements. Which ones fit Wiggins' definition of feedback?

- Your picture is so beautiful!
- You need to redo these three problems.
- I had trouble understanding what you were saying at the start of your speech.
- Next time, remember to run a spell-check before turning in your paper.
- Why did you choose those examples to prove your point?
- You'll need to run faster on the next lap to beat your best time.

Wiggins says that effective feedback is goal-referenced, tangible and transparent, actionable, user-friendly, timely, ongoing, and consistent.

- How well do you incorporate these seven keys to effective feedback in your teaching? What are some strategies you use to make sure your feedback includes these qualities?
- Which of these seven keys do you find most difficult to incorporate into your feedback? Choose one or two of these qualities and develop a plan for incorporating that quality into your feedback.

Feedback That Makes Students Think

In "How Am I Doing?" Jan Chappuis offers three examples of feedback that a teacher might give on a 10th grade social studies paper (see Figure 6.3). The first is an example of feedback that does all the thinking for the students; the second and third offer some guidance but require students to identify and correct their own errors. How do you respond to grammatical errors in student writing? How do you think your students would respond to the types of feedback Chappuis recommends?

Praiseworthy Praise

In "The Perils and Promises of Praise," Carol S. Dweck warns that praising students for their intelligence can have long-lasting negative effects, leading students to believe that academic success should come easily. Praise for effort, on the other hand, can encourage students to work hard and remain resilient when the work becomes difficult.

- Read Dweck's definition of the fixed mind-set and the growth mind-set (pp. 67–69). Which understanding of intelligence have you encountered most often in yourself, your colleagues, and your students? What effects of this mind-set have you seen in your students?
- Some students coast through school for years, successfully getting by with little effort. Others consistently work hard, but they continue to struggle. How can you help both types of students persevere when they reach academic roadblocks?

Assessments with Value

Teachers assess students each day, whether formally or informally. One of the most common means of informal assessment is asking questions during class. But in "The Right Questions, The Right Way," Dylan Wiliam notes that this time-honored classroom routine does not necessarily give teachers the information they need to plan upcoming lessons. When a teacher calls on a single volunteer to answer a question, all the teacher learns is what one willing student knows. How then can teachers make their in-class questioning routines more useful ways to assess learning of all their students?

- How do you usually question students? What do you learn from student responses to your questions? How might you make in-class questioning routines even more effective?
- In his article, Dylan Wiliam offers three strategies—no hands up, all-student response systems, and planning questions. Brent Duckor offers additional strategies in "Formative Assessment in Seven Good Moves." Have you used any of these strategies in your classroom? What was the result? If you haven't tried any of these strategies, which ones are you most interested in trying?

When at First They Don't Succeed...

If educators' goal is for students to learn, does it matter if it takes some students a little longer than others? Allowing students to redo assessments is one way to give students another chance if they haven't demonstrated mastery of the material on their first attempt. Myron Dueck explains how he got over his reluctance to allow retakes in "How I Broke My Rule and Learned to Give Retests."

- What's your current policy on offering redos and retakes? How did you arrive at this policy? Reflecting on the ideas Dueck presents, how might you change your policy? If you don't offer retakes, what steps might you take to introduce them in your classes? If you do, what new ideas do you have for making the practice more effective?
- Discuss some of the common objections to allowing redos and retakes. How might Dueck counter these objections? Which arguments—for and against—do you find most compelling?

Naomi Thiers is Associate Editor, *Educational Leadership*. **Teresa Preston** is a former Associate Editor of *Educational Leadership*.

EL Takeaways
On Formative Assessment

"Formative assessment is—or should be—the bridge or causeway between today's lesson and tomorrow's." — *Carol Ann Tomlinson*

"If educators view data as a liability simply because we don't know what to do with that data, we risk ignoring something that may help us. By viewing assessment as a system that gives us the power to feed up, feed back, and feed forward, we can avoid mistaking help for hindrance." — *Douglas Fisher and Nancy Frey*

"Using feedback isn't confined to a classroom. Consider its role in self-regulation and lifelong learning. We all stand to benefit from knowing when to seek feedback, how to seek it, and what to do with it when we get it." — *John Hattie*

"Feedback is only effective when it translates into a clear, positive message that students can hear." — *Susan M. Brookhart*

"Assessments can be a vital component in our efforts to improve education. But as long as we use them only as a means to rank schools and students, we will miss their most powerful benefits. We must focus instead on helping teachers change the way they use assessment results, improve the quality of their classroom assessments, and align their assessments with valued learning goals and state or district standards." — *Thomas R. Guskey*

"For informed teacher educators, formative assessment is more than a checklist of qualities or collection of activities. Rather, it's made up of a sequence of moves that invite a positive, ongoing relationship between teachers and their students." — *Brent Duckor*

Related ASCD Resources

At the time of publication, the following ASCD resources were available (ASCD stock numbers appear in parentheses). For up-to-date information about ASCD resources, go to www.ascd.org. You can search the complete archives of *Educational Leadership* at http://www.ascd.org/el.

ASCD EDge®

Exchange ideas and connect with other educators interested in math on the social networking site ASCD EDge at http://ascdedge.ascd.org.

Print Products

Assessment and Student Success in a Differentiated Classroom by Carol Ann Tomlinson & Tonya R. Moon (#108028)

Checking for Understanding: Formative Assessment Techniques for Your Classroom, 2nd edition (#115011) by Douglas Fisher and Nancy Frey

Formative Classroom Walkthroughs: How Principals and Teachers Collaborate to Raise Student Achievement by Connie M. Moss & Susan M. Brookhart (#115003)

How to Design Questions and Tasks to Assess Student Thinking by Susan M. Brookhart (#114014)

How to Make Decisions with Different Kinds of Student Assessment Data by Susan M. Brookhart (#116003)

The Data-Driven Classroom: How Do I Use Student Data to Improve My Instruction? (ASCD Arias) by Craig A. Mertler (#SF114082)

Transformative Assessment in Action: An Inside Look at Applying the Process by W. James Popham (#111008)

What Teachers Really Need to Know About Formative Assessment by Laura Greenstein (#110017)

Educational Leadership, November 2015: Doing Data Right (#116030)

Educational Leadership, September 2012: Feedback for Learning (#113032)

PD Online® Courses

Assessment and Student Success in a Differentiated Classroom (#PD14OC019M)

Assessment: Designing performance Assessments, 2nd Edition (#PD11OC108M)

Formative Assessment: Deepening Understanding (#PD11OC101M)

For more information: send e-mail to member@ascd.org; call 1-800-933-2723 or 703-578-9600, press 2; send a fax to 703-575-5400; or write to Information Services, ASCD, 1703 N. Beauregard St., Alexandria, VA 22311-1714 USA.

THE WHOLE CHILD

ASCD's Whole Child approach is an effort to transition from a focus on narrowly defined academic achievement to one that promotes the long-term development and success of all children. Through this approach, ASCD supports educators, families, community members, and policymakers as they move from a vision about educating the whole child to sustainable, collaborative actions.

On Formative Assessment: Readings from **Educational Leadership** relates to the **engaged, supported,** and **challenged** tenets.

WHOLE CHILD
TENETS

1 HEALTHY
Each student enters school healthy and learns about and practices a healthy lifestyle.

2 SAFE
Each student learns in an environment that is physically and emotionally safe for students and adults.

3 ENGAGED
Each student is actively engaged in learning and is connected to the school and broader community.

4 SUPPORTED
Each student has access to personalized learning and is supported by qualified, caring adults.

5 CHALLENGED
Each student is challenged academically and prepared for success in college or further study and for employment and participation in a global environment.

For more about the Whole Child approach, visit
www.wholechildeducation.org

LEARN. TEACH. LEAD.

CPSIA information can be obtained at www.ICGtesting.com
Printed in the USA
BVOW06s0526190916

462552BV00029B/239/P

9 781416 622925